# GETTING
## TO
# BARTLETT STREET

OUR 25-YEAR QUEST
*to* LEVEL *the* PLAYING FIELD
*in* EDUCATION

## Joe AND Carol Reich

 FEBRUARY BOOKS

http://februarybooks.com

Library of Congress Control Number: 2012937006

Reich, Joe and Carol
*Getting to Bartlett Street: Our 25-Year Quest to Level
the Playing Field in Education*

Joe and Carol Reich.—1st edition

ISBNs:
978-0-9849543-0-8 (hardcover)
978-0-9849543-2-2 (electronic)

Printed in the United State of America

February Books are distributed to the trade by
Consortium Book Sales & Distribution
Phone: 800-283-3572 / SAN 631-760X

*Jacket design by Thomas Beck Stvan*
*Book design by Casey Hampton*

*Life is lived forward but understood backward*
*if you are still around to comprehend it.*

—SØREN KIERKEGAARD

# CONTENTS

# BY JOEL KLEIN

Among other things, this book is timely. It comes at a critical moment for public school reform in America. As the nation continues to struggle with the worst economic crisis it has faced since the Great Depression, there is a gathering consensus that our current level of educational attainment is not remotely adequate for the demands of a high-tech, global economy—an economy that requires many more knowledge workers than it used to, and one that can also look to new, emerging economies to find the workers it needs. Faced with an unemployment and underemployment rate of more than 15 percent, accompanied by a significant across-the-board decline in real wages for many workers, the divide in America between the haves and have-nots is becoming increasingly acute, and now threatens the values that hold us together as a nation. Whatever else, one thing seems obvious: we need to educate our future workforce to a very different degree or our problems will only intensify. This is serious stuff.

Unfortunately, despite a shared recognition about the need to dramatically improve public education, there remains sharp disagreement about how best to do that. The policies pushed by the reform movement—based largely on bringing accountability and choice to the monopoly-run, adult-interest-driven status quo—have enjoyed a measure of success during the past decade. But, to be candid, the system still hasn't changed much. Schools, along with those who work in them, rarely pay the price of failure, and for most families in America school choice is nonexistent.

First, let's recognize some places that have demonstrated how real change and improvement are achievable: Florida, which under Governor Jeb Bush's leadership adopted aggressive reforms, such as putting a letter grade on all schools and denying promotion to third-graders who can't read; and New Orleans, which, in response to the destruction of the old public school system wrought by Hurricane Katrina, adopted an all-choice system in which three-quarters of the schools are now independent charter schools. But despite these (and other) examples of success, the forces defending the largely unaltered status quo continue to resist meaningful change, arguing that what the system really needs is more resources and, strangely, less accountability and choice.

Into this debate now sail Joe and Carol Reich, two remarkable people from whom, all things considered, one would never have expected to hear. School reform is messy, involving highly charged, sometimes very ugly politics, which often get played out in some of the poorest, most dangerous parts of our urban landscapes. The Reiches, by contrast, are elegant and, yes, like their name is pronounced, rich. But for reasons that will become apparent to readers of this book, they have too much gratitude to this country, too fine a sense of equity and fairness, and too deep a belief in the power of education to transform even the most challenged life, to sit this fight out. So, having been exposed to sixty underprivileged children to whom they guaranteed college scholarships through the "I Have A Dream" Foundation, the Reiches decided to open up their own public school in one of New York's most impoverished communities—South Williamsburg, Brooklyn—which is divided largely between an immigrant Hispanic community and an orthodox Jewish community.

Nothing like this had ever previously happened in the city. Until the Reiches, it was axiomatic that the schools were run exclusively by the Board of Education. Not surprisingly, then, from day one, the attitude of everyone involved in the school system—the big shots, the bureaucrats, and the union—was that this must be a joke. But Joe and Carol didn't think it was a laughing matter. The odyssey they describe is a testament to their extraordinary fortitude. It is also, sadly, a testament to the power of the "blob"—the term used to describe the protectors of the monopoly public school system—to resist outside "encroachment," or any form of innovation, for that matter, at all costs. The late Steve Jobs, a fierce critic of the public school system, repeatedly analogized the public schools to deeply entrenched business monopolies, like AT&T when it controlled the entire telephone system. Jobs noted, "I remember seeing a bumper sticker with the Bell logo on it and it saying, 'We don't care. We don't have to.' And that's what monopoly is. That's what IBM was in their day. And that's certainly what the public school system is. They don't have to care."

But Joe and Carol Reich did care—cared so much that they fought through the extraordinary resistance and indifference that is hard to describe to anyone who hasn't been directly exposed to the blob. The beneficiaries are not just the families who chose to have their kids attend the Reiches' two schools in Brooklyn, but literally tens of thousands of families whose kids go to charter schools throughout the city—schools that might never have existed if it weren't for the Reiches' pathbreaking efforts. That is the story they chronicle in this deeply moving book, a story of profound change brought about by a couple of miscast outsiders who just didn't know how to take no for an answer.

Before talking about the story and its impact, let me say a word about the Reiches. Over the past decade, I have come to know them well. They are friends that I admire and love. As any reader of this book will see, they care deeply about others, especially those who are less fortunate. When they describe the kids from the "I Have A Dream" program (they call them "our Dreamers") and when they refer to the kids who attend their schools, they talk of them as if they were literally their own children. This reflects an emotional attachment that speaks volumes about the Reiches' humanity, which is matched by the pointed simplicity of the values that animate both of them. Why did they do it? Why did they keep going despite the impossible odds and the endless ridiculous push back? The answer is served up in what I believe to be the most important words in the book:

> Families of means can afford to send their children to private schools or relocate to a neighborhood of affluence where the public schools have greater resources. The poor cannot. We recoiled against this injustice. We made it our own struggle.

To me, these words strike at the core of the current injustice inherent in public education. When I was chancellor in New York City, I would always ask people if they would let me assign their child to any of the public schools in the city. No one said yes, and most, when pressed, said they would only allow their kids to go to a third or so of the city's schools. Who should go to the others, I would ask? The answer was, "Other people's children!"

Today in New York City, because of the work that Joe and Carol Reich started more than twenty years ago, many more families in high-poverty communities have a choice as to where they will send their kids. Sparked by the work of the Reiches and others, like Seymour Fliegel and his team at the Center for Educational Innovation,

New York State passed a charter school law in 1998, allowing for the first time the potential for a real alternative to the public schools. As the Reiches explain, charter schools are privately operated (typically not-for-profit) schools that admit kids by lottery and receive public funding to provide them with a free education. They are subjected to the same testing and other accountability standards as the public schools, and can be, and have been, shut down for nonperformance or financial irregularities.

In many school districts in America today, charter schools, while authorized, are fiercely resisted, typically by superintendents, school boards, and unions. This trinity is nearly impossible to overcome. But in New York City, because of Mayor Michael Bloomberg's leadership, the support of the philanthropic community, and the commitment of some of the nation's best multi-charter operators, charter schools have thrived. They now number 136, which amounts to almost 10 percent of all the public schools in the city. And their impact on high-poverty communities, where they tend to be clustered—like northern Manhattan, the South Bronx, and central Brooklyn—is even greater.

There is a raging debate in the education literature about whether charters do better or worse than public schools as a whole. As the Reiches point out, there are a lot of poor charters out there, and some cut corners by not admitting, or discharging, kids that are especially difficult to educate. But the research now makes clear that charter schools in New York City are significantly outperforming the other public schools. Just as important, I would argue, the parents in the city are voting with their feet. For the school year that started in September 2011, there were a total of almost thirteen thousand new charter seats available across the city, for which sixty-four thousand families applied. That is a remarkable number, by any measure. It speaks volumes about the fact that, contrary to conventional opinion, parents in even the most challenged communities will become active and involved consumers of educational services for their children if they are given real choices. Remember, not a single one of the sixty-four thousand was required to apply to a charter school; on the contrary, they each were assigned to a community school that their children could attend. But they wanted something better for their kids, so they took the time to apply to one or more charter schools, knowing the odds would be against them, but nevertheless hoping their kid would be lucky enough to get a better education than the one he would have received at the public school in his community.

What's sad, as the Reiches point out, is that, despite the demonstrated success of charter schools, as well as the enormous demand for them in New York City, there is still enormous resistance to their expansion. The teachers' union has sued the city time and again to block them. In part, that's because, unlike the public schools, which must be unionized, the charters overwhelmingly choose to be non-union. In addition, the current workforce in the public schools doesn't like the competition that the charters provide: if kids leave the traditional public schools for the charters, fewer employees will be needed, and the unions, when push comes to shove, choose to protect jobs.

In the end, I suspect, the parents will prevail. Those sixty-four thousand applicants won't be denied and, as a political force, they are formidable. They have learned something very important: because their kids grow up poor and often face very difficult challenges doesn't mean they can't be well educated. For far too long, the failures of the public schools have been blamed on everything—including the kids—but not on the schools. Well, now parents increasingly know better.

And for that, those parents, and many more throughout our nation, owe a debt of gratitude to a couple of people they have never heard of: Joe and Carol Reich. If you have any doubt that an individual can change the world for the better, read this book. Against all odds, and in the face of persistent, unyielding naysayers, these two people led a revolution in education in the largest school district in the country. In the words of my favorite song from the Broadway show *A Little Night Music,* "Isn't it Reich?"

# TO GIRLS LIKE INGRID

Ingrid Aponte was going to become a doctor. At least this is what she'd been telling herself, day after day, since the time she was just eleven years old. It didn't matter that the odds seemed stacked against her, or that most of the children who grew up like she did—in the low-income community of South Williamsburg, Brooklyn in the mid-1980s—didn't make it to high school graduation, let alone to medical school. It didn't even matter that, as she was reminded so often, she was just a poor Puerto Rican girl living in the ghetto. She was going to do everything she could to make it happen—work hard at school, stay off the corners, and, in the meantime, pray as hard as she could for a little extra luck.

After all, taking care of people was something she loved to do, and she did it well. She had always known she was a skilled caregiver, but it was an experience she had at the age of twelve that erased any doubt on this matter, and sealed her dream to be a doctor. One day, after leaving the crowded apartment she shared with her mother, stepfather, and three younger siblings, she noticed a man standing across the street. It looked as if he'd cut his hand or arm—both were bleeding profusely, and he was crying for help. None of the adults gathered on the nearby corner seemed interested. All they ever seemed interested in were the little bags of white powder they sold all hours of the day and night.

Ingrid ran across the street before realizing she didn't have anything with which to help this man. Without hesitating, she ripped her shirt, and used the fabric to tightly tie his wound, and stem the flow of blood. The look of gratitude this man gave her afterward was like nothing she'd really seen before. She knew she had done something heroic, and she loved how it felt to be able to ease this man's suffering. She began to read what she could about medicine. When her uncle told her about a friend of his who worked at a pediatric emergency room in the Bronx, Ingrid begged to be introduced to this doctor. He soon agreed that she could come to the hospital—where he worked the overnight shift in the ER—and shadow him.

It took her more than an hour on the subway to reach the Bronx in time for the 8:00 p.m. shift. For nearly twelve hours, Ingrid, now thirteen, worked side by side with the team of emergency room doctors. She watched as they wrapped a deep gash in a baby's head, set broken limbs, and tended to the needs of child after child with a true sense of empathy and kindness—a true sense of grace. The next morning, after eating her breakfast with the doctors in the cafeteria at 6:00 a.m., she rushed back to Williamsburg, where she was a just about to enter the seventh grade at Junior High School 50.

She wasn't thrilled about going to JHS 50—at times, the halls of the school felt no safer than the street corners—but she didn't have any other choice. Despite her mother's hope that Ingrid get every opportunity available to her, her stepfather would never have agreed to pay for an education at a better school. His only real voiced concern was that she show up on time for work at the fast-food restaurant he owned on the Lower East Side of Manhattan, where, each weekend since she was nine, she and her younger brother worked from the time the restaurant opened until it closed. So many times—at work at the restaurant, after hearing of another shooting in a building around the corner, after seeing another girl her age get pregnant and leave school—Ingrid nearly gave up the idea that she could escape this life, that she could ever leave South Williamsburg and become a doctor. Even if she did work hard and get good grades, her stepfather would never pay for college. Maybe she really was nothing.

And then the day came when a man named Gino Maldonado arrived at her apartment, asking to speak to Ingrid and her mother. He worked at El Puente, a community organization not too far from their home, and he explained that as a member of the graduating class of sixth graders at PS 17, Ingrid had been chosen to be part of the "I Have A Dream" program. Through this program, her college tuition would be paid for. All she had to do was finish high school. Ingrid had a hard time believing the words Gino was telling her and for the next few days, she was sure it was all a dream—after all, things like that didn't happen to girls like her. But then Gino called again, and told her mother that Ingrid had to be at the auditorium of JHS 50 on a specific night in September. When Ingrid entered the auditorium that evening alongside her mother, she saw a group of adults she didn't recognize standing on the stage. After the students and their parents took their seats, one of the men on stage started to speak. Ingrid listened as closely as she could.

"If you graduate from high school, we will pay for your college tuition," the man said.

Most of the students around her seemed confused. Others just seemed bored. Ingrid felt dizzy with excitement. Maybe it *was* true.

She walked out of the auditorium that evening with her head in the clouds. She knew this was the moment she'd been praying for. That night at home, she came to believe something else: Good things *could* happen to girls like her. And maybe dreams really could come true.

# PART
# 1

# PURE *BESHERT*

## *JOE*

My wife Carol and I were the people on the stage that day, and while it's been wonderful to hear students like Ingrid speak of their appreciation for the program we became involved in, it truly has been our privilege to do this work, and get to know so many people who've been such an inspiration to us.

I first learned about the I Have A Dream Foundation on June 21, 1987, while reading the *New York Times*. An article that day featured the work of Eugene M. Lang, a successful entrepreneur who had attended public schools in New York during the Great Depression. A few years earlier, Gene had been invited to speak to students at PS 121, the grammar school in East Harlem he'd attended fifty years earlier. He arrived at his former school that day prepared to impart to the students a simple message: if you work hard in life, you're bound to succeed. But when he walked into the struggling school and took in his surroundings, he began to understand the challenges many of the students there faced. The speech he had prepared felt ill-suited to the realities. After all, how could he stand in front of a room full of students where three-quarters of the graduating eighth graders would never go on to finish high school, and tell them that all they needed to do was to work hard?

He scrapped that speech and the announcement he ended up making that day surprised every one of the sixty-one students present, not to mention Gene himself. "Don't think you can't go to college," he told the packed classroom. "I promise that if you finish high school, I will provide you a scholarship so you can." Gene kept his promise and not only did he pay for each student's college tuition when the time came, he remained an ongoing presence in their lives. In 1986, Gene turned his vision into the "I Have A Dream" Foundation, which showed the way for others looking to make an impact in the lives of kids who might otherwise have been without hope for their future.

I was so pleased to come across the article that morning. By the time I finished reading it, I knew I might have found a solution to a nagging desire I'd had for some years: to help others have the same opportunities Carol and I had had and that we'd been able to provide for our three daughters. In so many ways, I could not have stumbled upon this article at a better time in my life.

I was born in Pittsburgh on December 16, 1934, but I have come to believe that my life didn't truly begin until Sunday, November 8, 1953, at about 6:00 p.m. This was the moment when I entered Clara Dickson Hall at Cornell University to pick up my blind date, a seventeen-year-old freshman from Chicago named Carol Friedman. I still remember every detail of that evening as if it were yesterday. Carol was wearing a fuzzy gray coat and at the Sunnyside Restaurant, where we went for dinner along with two other couples, she ordered chicken in a basket. After listening to all of the New Yorkers that surrounded me at Cornell, her heavy Midwestern accent sounded melodious to me, and the fact that she ordered the least expensive item on the menu told me even more about the kind of person she was. Afterward, we went to see the movie *Shane*, starring Alan Ladd. I could hardly take my eyes off her as we sat outside her dorm in one of my friends' cars, talking until exactly 10:30 p.m., when she had to go inside to make her curfew.

There's a Yiddish word, *beshert,* that means something fated or ordained to be, and my initial attraction to her felt like nothing less than pure *beshert.* To my good fortune, Carol felt the same way and we were married two years later, on November 11, 1955 at the Belden-Stratford Hotel in Lincoln Park, on the Near North Side of Chicago. At the time, the US military required service of every male. I had two options: get drafted into the Army or volunteer to serve in another branch of the military. I chose the latter and applied to the Navy Officer Candidate School in Newport, Rhode Island. Carol's father, Dr. Townsend Friedman, had served in the navy during World War II. I was hoping this might soften Dr. Friedman's opposition to the idea of his daughter marrying a penniless twenty-year-old with, at best, an uncertain future.

About a year after we were married, in December 1956 we found out that Carol was pregnant. To be frank, the news terrified us. We knew that we wanted children, but we were not prepared to start a family so early into our marriage. Carol was barely twenty-one years old at the time and I was about to go to sea for six months on an aircraft carrier in the Far East. But, despite the fear we felt, I knew that Carol and I would find a way. After all, we were young and in love—we could handle anything.

We lost that baby a month later in January. It was a devastating experience for us, and we were both grief-stricken. We were further tested two months later when Carol's father died suddenly of a heart attack four weeks before I was due to leave for the Western Pacific for six months on an aircraft carrier. After my return we became determined to become parents as soon as possible. But in the ensuing years, Carol suffered two more miscarriages. After that, we seemed unable to conceive. The various fertility technologies prevalent today did not exist then and by mid-1959, we abandoned the idea of having our own biological child.

I had finished my three years in the navy by this time and was pursuing an MBA at Stanford University, in Palo Alto, California. Here, we started the lengthy process of adoption in California. In September 1959, after having completed the process and gotten approval from a social worker, we were informed that were to receive a baby in six weeks! We were thrilled. All that remained was to obtain a certificate from Carol's doctor attesting to our inability to have a child by natural means. We went to her gynecologist, a wonderful, courtly gentleman named Pendleton Tompkins, who, after examining Carol, said he could not sign the form.

Why?

She was eight weeks pregnant.

We tried to convince him to sign the paper anyway—after all, after three miscarriages, we were anything but confident that this pregnancy would go to term—but he refused. The pregnancy was not difficult, but we continued to be fearful that we could lose this baby as well. But lo and behold, seven months later, Deborah Ann Reich was born. When we asked Dr. Tompkins about the prospect of more children, he advised us that it would likely take us a few more years to conceive again. One year and three days later, we proved him wrong with the arrival of Marcia Ellen Reich in Houston, Texas, where I had found a job with Continental Oil Company after completing my MBA. My goal had been to be in the investment field in New York City. In June 1961, I took a job in New York at Donaldson, Lufkin & Jenrette (DLJ), a new Wall Street firm.

Our third and final child, Janet, was born in August 1967 in New York City. At DLJ none of the firm's founders was over thirty, and there were very few rules. We made it up as we went along. It was very exciting, at least for a while. Eventually, a major disagreement developed over the division of ownership at the firm. I, along with one of my colleagues Oscar Tang, thought it was time to adjust the ownership to reflect the increasing contribution of the younger partners. The disagreement couldn't be resolved and so, in 1968, Oscar and I decided to go off on our own, creating the firm, Reich & Tang (R&T).

Our company did not get off to a great start. The 1970s were a very difficult time in the financial world. Our original business was managing equity portfolios for pension funds and endowments. The financial downturn, coupled with the passage of the Employee Retirement Income Security Act of 1974 (ERISA), made it difficult for small firms to gain accounts to manage. With our continued existence in doubt we had little choice but to innovate. R&T became one of the pioneers in the field of money market funds in 1974. These funds enabled small savers to pool their funds and earn returns nearly equal to the big investors, something hitherto impossible because prohibited by a Federal Reserve regulation supported by the banks and brokers limiting interest paid to small savers and investors. This regulation greatly benefited the banks and brokers and at the expense of small savers and investors. We encountered a small, well-organized opposition from defenders of the status quo. This opposition was a foreshadowing of the opposition Carol and I faced in education reform. R&T developed a niche and an aptitude in this field, which started slowly. However it was exciting work and it also felt good. When interest rates rose again in 1978, the business began to grow very rapidly. For nearly twenty years, I worked hard at R&T, and by the mid-1980s, I was growing bored. I'd made a lot of money, and it was coming to feel as if we had enough. Carol and I had been able to provide a comfortable life for our daughters, and we were far wealthier than we had ever expected when we were first married. Why did I need any more? Instead, at the age of fifty-two, I was beginning to think more seriously about the years ahead of me, and how I wanted to spend them. I knew it wasn't in the pursuit of additional wealth. I remember one very specific, and very important, moment. At our firm, I was usually the person who gave our presentation to the potential clients we were courting, and in time, I'd gotten quite good at it. One day in late 1986, I was in the midst of a presentation to a university endowment when I realized I could not remember the name of the university or the size of the fund. The work, once fascinating to me, had become rote. The worst part, perhaps, was that despite my not remembering who the client was, we still got the business.

It was about this time that I recalled a letter Carol had written to me once nearly thirty years earlier. Soon after we married, the navy sent me away for six months. The only way we could communicate during this long time apart was through letters, and we wrote to each other every single day. In one letter—dated August 20, 1957—Carol wrote to me about an idea I'd shared with her: I wanted to go to business school.

"I developed a new thought," my young wife wrote. "I think it strange that the prime concern of a business school education is the monetary return it will bring. Perhaps I'm an ivory tower-ite, but higher education should involve something more than that. I can almost understand a degree in history or literature more. What I'm trying to say is, are you sure that business school is what you want? I don't deny that I'd love to buy my clothes at Bergdorf, but that is not a prime concern. I hate today's idea of success—only the monetary return has any importance. I don't want this to happen. I don't care how long it takes you to find yourself, since that's the most important thing."

I'd kept all of Carol's letters (and she'd kept all of mine) and re-reading it around that time, I knew I was on the very path that Carol had feared for me so many years earlier. Because while the investment world truly had engaged and excited me in the beginning, I had lost my passion for it. I had been left with wealth, but that no longer felt like enough. In the meantime, I admired what Carol was doing. She had become the first female chair of the Lexington School for the Deaf, the largest school for deaf students in New York State, which had been founded in 1864. Her job was both demanding and rewarding. As I listened to her stories and observed the ways she was able to mold a school and enrich the lives of students through education, I knew I wanted to spend my time doing something that felt equally challenging and worthwhile.

So I made a decision: I was going to leave R&T. The timing was, at least according to most people I knew, insane. Our firm was just going public and staying put would have meant far greater riches.

I had no regrets about walking away from the firm. But that's not to say I had a clear plan for what was to come next. Many of my colleagues expressed their concern and one day I received a call from good friend.

"What are you going to *do* now, Joe?" he asked me.

I had to think about it for a while. "I don't have a clue," I said finally.

"That sounds really stupid," my friend said laughing, and I can't say I disagreed.

"Well, how about this?" I answered. "I'm going to spend a third of my time teaching, a third of my time investing, and a third of my time giving our money away."

This time, my friend didn't laugh.

"That sounds like a rich and satisfying way to spend your time," he said.

Before long, I had made two of my three goals happen. I took a position as an adjunct professor at Columbia Business School, creating and teaching a course in entrepreneurship. The work was interesting, but I could never quite escape the feeling that there had to be a lot of other people who could teach a course like that as well as I could. I also did the investing part, which came easily enough. But I was having a hard time with my philanthropic goals. I knew I wanted to do more than simply write a check to a good cause. Instead, I was committed to combining our financial resources with my time to achieve something truly meaningful and worthwhile.

That was my mind-set when I first went to talk to Gene Lang about the "I Have A Dream" program. I'd called him as soon as I finished reading the article, and he had invited me to his Manhattan office to talk. Even on my way over to meet him, I didn't truly understand what kind of commitment I might be taking on.

Gene is a hard man to say no to, and within minutes, I was on board with a commitment to support the college education of sixty students. When Gene asked me where I'd choose the students from, I responded I'd find a public school in West Virginia. My family had moved from Pittsburgh to West Virginia in 1949, when I was fourteen years old. I attended Charleston High School from 1949 to 1951—at a time when schools were still segregated, and West Virginia schools ranked forty-seventh out of forty-eight in the country. I was a good student, but my education was abysmal, in Charleston as well as in Pittsburgh. At my elementary school, the principal regularly beat the students for misbehaving, and the teachers were not much kinder. I couldn't wait for the school day to end, when I'd rush home and listen to Edward R. Murrow reporting from London and study the statistics of the latest Pittsburgh Pirates game. (I was in the bleachers at Forbes Field on May 15, 1947 on the day that Jackie Robinson played his first game in Pittsburgh. My friend Richard Thorpe and I were the only two white people in the right field bleachers, which were completely full even though Forbes Field itself was two thirds empty. Without realizing it I was seeing segregation in operation. Although only 12 years old, I knew something was wrong with that scene. It's a day I will never forget.) "Oh, so you are going to move back to West Virginia?" Gene asked.

I was confused, and afraid that I'd said something to mislead him. "No," I responded. "We live here."

"Joe," Gene said, with a hint of exaggerated patience. "This is a job. You are going to be working with these kids. It will consume you."

And so I decided: I (and hopefully Carol) would sponsor a class in New York. After all, if I was going to do this, I wanted to do it right.

When I arrived home that evening, I couldn't wait to tell Carol about my plan.

"You want to do *what?*" my wife asked, giving me the look I'd grown more than accustomed to during the past thirty-two years of our marriage.

Her immediate concern was that we would be getting to the kids too late to truly impact their lives. Their development would be too far along already and they would be too set in their ways. It would never work to try to change their lives that far.

"You don't understand!" I had the audacity to say to my wife—a woman with a PhD in developmental psychology and the president of a school. I went on to explain that with a good plan like I had used in business, and clear thinking, we'd succeed in helping these kids succeed.

I know Carol, and I therefore also know that in that moment, she was working very hard to resist the urge to laugh out loud. Business plan? With kids?

I took her hand. "Let's do it anyway, OK?"

"OK, let's," she said. "But remember what I said: It might be too late. It might not work."

Over the next few weeks, Carol and I spent a lot of time discussing where in New York we'd focus our efforts. Our main objective was to find a community that really needed our support, as well as one with an established community based organization that could help us serve the students and through which we could manage the program.

We found exactly what we were looking for in South Williamsburg, Brooklyn.

Anybody familiar with the Williamsburg of today knows it to be a tony, high-priced neighborhood of luxury condos, high-end boutiques, and trendy restaurants. But this was hardly the scene just twenty-five years ago, when the neighborhood was rife with poverty and crime. A map of the city at the time even labeled this area as a *dead zone:* a term used to designate incredibly impoverished communities. Here in the dead zone, residents from Puerto Rico, the Dominican Republic, and other Latin American countries lived side by side with a large population of Satmar Hasidic Jews who had begun to settle in the area in the years after World War II. The streets surrounding the local junior high school—JHS 50—served as an uneasy buffer between the two communities.

In our search, we had discovered El Puente, a community center on South Fourth Street in South Williamsburg founded in 1982 by an activist named Luis Garden Acosta. Luis had a colorful, radical past. He had been part of an organization that called itself the Young Lords, which sounded to us like something straight out of *West Side Story.* He had gone on to study at Harvard Medical School. We thought El Puente was our best chance for a local organization that had credibility in the community, and our plan was to pay them to house and help manage our "I Have A Dream" program.

When we first met him, Luis was enthusiastic about the program, but our sense was that he believed we'd come in, contribute some money and return to the Upper East Side of Manhattan. He expected to see us maybe once a year. He thought we would be totally disengaged and removed.

He thought wrong.

Through Luis, we met Gino Maldonado, a cofounder of El Puente, who we hired as project coordinator to help us manage the program. With his assistance, we identified the sixty sixth-graders who had graduated in June from PS 17, and agreed that El Puente would be the home base for the different activities we would be organizing for our Dreamers. Gino, along with a young Barnard student named Elizabeth Guzman, who was from the neighborhood, continued to meet with each of the sixty kids and their families. They talked to them one-on-one to see if they had any questions and understood the program. They knew some of the kids already, but many they were meeting for the first time.

Despite the crumbling buildings and the groups of drug dealers we passed on the way, Carol and I felt hopeful and expectant when we arrived at JHS 50 early on that chilly evening in September 1987 to meet our Dreamers for the first time. We were shown to a dark and somewhat dank auditorium for the gathering of our sixty students. I realized that this was the first time I had ever set foot in a New York City public school. I had made a decision from the heart, not availing myself of the analytical skills that had served me so well in business. It felt odd but very right. With Gene at our side, we made our pledge. The kids shifted uneasily, not sure what to make of us or what we were offering. And really, how could they be? Attending college was not a goal many of them had been encouraged to pursue. The idea that we would pay their tuition probably made little sense to them. No one listening to our promise—and I have to include ourselves in this—could have possibly understood the full significance of the commitment we were making.

When the event finished, Carol and I blinked our way back into the softening light of evening. We stood on the sidewalk, feeling elated. In the car on the way home, my head swelled with excitement about all the things we could do with our Dreamers. Carol was equally excited, but I knew that she also remained concerned that the efforts we were making, not to mention the financial commitment—we'd eventually spend more than one million dollars on our Dreamers—would be futile. "I don't know," she said to me later that evening. "I still think we may be getting to these kids too late. We might not be able to do enough." I tried not to share her concerns. After all, we had gone through a lot during, at that time, more than thirty years of marriage: our early years of making very little money while financing my graduate education at Stanford and eventually her PhD; starting a very successful business; and raising three wonderful daughters, all while maintaining a very happy marriage, and a strong partnership. I think it was fair to say that we had a lot of experience getting difficult things done.

This time would be no different.

Over the next several months, we became so involved with the program, and spent so much time at El Puente, that Luis and the Dreamers took to calling our program "I Have a Nightmare." Getting a firsthand look at the schooling our Dreamers were getting was a real eye-opener for us. Most of them were several years behind grade level, and JHS 50 was mired in a school district controlled by a bureaucracy that we later discovered was built on criminality. This system may have worked for the adults it employed, but it was clearly working against the children. Lacking choice in education, they seemed to have little opportunity to ever escape the dead zone.

To make matters far worse, we soon realized that nothing we were doing to help give our kids a good education could undo the realities of their lives when the school day ended. We got to know students like Juanita* and James*. When we asked Juanita what she wanted to be when she grew up, she couldn't think of one response.

Nobody had ever told her that she had any sort of choice in that. James lived in an apartment with his mother, who was mentally ill and oftentimes violent. His father had left the family long ago to pursue a full-time drug habit. We'd see the scene that the students had to pass each day on their way to JHS 50: crack dealers on each corner, asking the students if they wanted some "ice."

The more we got to know our kids, the more we began to realize that we wanted to do more than simply pay for their eventual college tuition. Having to spend so much time worrying about the gunshots they heard day and night, the dirty needles they walked over on the sidewalk, and their parents' endless struggle to earn enough money for food, rent, and clothes, how could we expect them to also worry about homework and keeping good grades? Working with El Puente, we developed an array of ancillary programs for our Dreamers, hoping to expose them to new, enriching experiences. We set up a mentoring program, through which many of my former colleagues from the financial world volunteered to help our students. If certain students decided that they wanted to apply to a private high school, when the time came we helped them with their application, and paid the tuition. When someone like Ingrid Aponte told us of a summer archeological camp in Colorado, and we saw how eager she was to attend, we paid for that as well. When it came time to apply to college, we enrolled every one of our Dreamers into SAT preparation classes.

We saw the value of exposing our Dreamers not just to new experiences, but to new environments, so we also began to organize trips to many places they'd never been before: western Massachusetts, for a skiing weekend; Lime Rock Park, a motor-sports venue in Lakeville, Connecticut; Six Flags amusement park. We may have only been a few hours away from Williamsburg, but by the look on their faces, they had dropped their street wariness and were joyful.

In the years that have passed since we got involved with the IHAD program, our students have intermittently come and gone in our lives. Admittedly, some struggled and never made it to high school graduation. Others far exceeded our expectations, and we are so proud of them: of people like Sandra Martinez*, who graduated from Baruch College with a degree in business administration in finance. Roberto Reyes, who attended Saint Ann's School, one of the most prestigious high schools in New York City, and then went on to graduate from Wesleyan University and, eventually, earn his master's in Education from Columbia University. Celia Ortiz*, who graduated from our alma mater, Cornell University, went on to receive her medical degree, and is today a practicing psychiatrist. Two of our students even married each other and remain married today, seventeen years later!

As for Ingrid Aponte? She took care of her end of the bargain. She graduated from high school and was granted a scholarship to the University at Buffalo. We happily took care of the expenses not covered by the scholarship. After graduating, she attended medical school in Peru, and today Ingrid Herrera M.D, is a wife, a mother, and a practicing physician in the Midwest. "At times I wasn't sure it would actually happen," she recently told us. "But it did. I really am living my dream."

# TWO

# BEGINNING WITH CHILDREN

## CAROL

Despite the wonderful and encouraging progress Joe and I observed with students like Ingrid, Sandra, and Celia, I could never quite shake my initial belief that to *truly* have a lasting impact, we had to reach kids earlier than junior high school. This belief was further cemented about a year later, when Joe and I had an experience with our Dreamers that neither one of us will ever forget. It was a sunny afternoon in the spring of 1988, late into our first year of working with our Dreamers. We were at JHS 50 for an event with the students. Afterward, Joe and I were standing on the sidewalk outside when we inadvertently overheard a conversation among a small group of adults from the school standing nearby. Clearly not having noticed the two of us, they began to talk in harsh, agitated tones about the gathering. Apparently, these adults thought we were foolish and misguided to be offering to send the sixty-one Dreamers to college. It was the words of one woman who spoke next that made us both catch our breaths.

"Why would anyone do that for *this garbage?*" she asked the group. "They're never going to amount to anything."

We immediately turned to look at each other, each silently asking the same question: *Had we heard the words right?* Joe's face was frozen in a look of surprise and horror. *Garbage?* What would cause a person to think and talk about children in such a way? It never occurred to me that anything about what that woman said was accurate, but over and over again throughout the next several weeks, that word—*garbage*—echoed in my head. Every time I brought it up to Joe, we said the same thing: maybe it's time to do something more. It was Joe's idea that we explore the idea of opening a school, and as soon as he suggested it to me I was my often hesitant self. That's not to say I wasn't totally skeptical about our chances of actually accomplishing it, but creating a school, and designing an education program that could enrich the lives of children in poverty, was something I knew we had to try. Would we succeed? Who knew, but I was sure we'd give it our best shot.

I have always been intrigued by education, which might be due to the fact that, unlike my husband, who succeeded despite his early educational experiences, I had what I think was a dream of an education. This started even before I entered school, with my father, who instilled in me a great love of learning. He loved to buy me books and from the moment I learned to read, I could usually be found behind a book. To this day, one of the favorite things I own is an early edition of the *The Complete Works of William Shakespeare* illustrated by Rockwell Kent. My father gave this to me for my first birthday.

My father also worked hard to expose me to the world. He was a doctor and on weekends he would take me with him to make house calls on the South Side of Chicago, where the Mississippi migration stopped. There I was, a little girl of seven or eight, visiting families who were stuck in poverty, living in houses that were nothing more than four stories of wooden fire traps with attached porches. What I was seeing was part of the Great Migration and the people who did it wanted better lives.

There is an ancient Hebrew expression, *tikkun olam*, that means: it's your job to make the world a better place than you found it. I didn't know that phrase at the time, but my father taught me its meaning in his own way. "You see this, Carol?" he'd ask me during these house calls, after long conversations with his patients who talked about how much they struggled to make ends meet, to even just get by. "This is wrong, and it's all of our responsibility to fix."

My mother had a different opinion on these matters. This was, after all, the 1940s, and she felt that as a girl, my focus should be on learning how to develop my skills at attracting boys, rather than on my intellect and social conscience. Like most women her age, her education didn't extend beyond high school, and she couldn't seem to understand why I wouldn't be happy to just settle for the same.

A lot of schools talk about being progressive, but my school on the South Side of Chicago, the University of Chicago Laboratory Schools, really was. John Dewey, the influential progressive educator and philosopher, had established the Lab late in the nineteenth century to function as a laboratory to test his ideas about education. These could be summed up by his belief that "a child is a social being," with all that entails, and that "the object and reward of learning is continued capacity for growth."

Dewey was a true visionary. The *New York Times* would later describe my school in Hyde Park as "a Gothic pile across the street from the University of Chicago," and that was about right. It *was* a Gothic pile. It was also a great school, which was why my father decided to send me there. At the time, it was very experimental, just half a generation away from its inception, and unlike at the segregated West Virginia schools of Joe's experience, we had children of all kinds, colors, and races. I learned very early that race was not destiny.

My sixth-grade teacher at the Lab School brought in Langston Hughes to teach poetry. The class had already been reading Hughes's poetry, and here was the man himself, right in front of us, gentle and commanding and eloquent all at once. Enrico Fermi, known for his work on the first nuclear reactor, came in to teach us physics, the subject for which he'd won the Nobel Prize in 1938. His son was in the class and sat right next to me. (I had never seen an Italian boy before.) It's safe to say I loved every minute I spent at the Lab School.

But, despite all of this, my mother remained worried that I was becoming too intellectual (*savage* was the word she preferred to use). So as part of her plan to make me over, she took away my books and gave me, instead, a charge account at the local Walgreens soda fountain in Chicago, hoping I would spend my time there trying to attract the attention of the young men and enrolled me in a girls' four-year finishing school, which I found so deathly boring I couldn't leave fast enough. The plan was less than a resounding success. Taking the term *finishing* literally, I graduated in three years.

When I arrived at Cornell in the fall of 1953, it was just one of two coed universities in the Ivy League. This made the university progressive for its time, but only to an extent. More than 80 percent of the student population was male and the female students were not always treated with total equality. For example, as women, we were all required to learn the most efficient way to iron a man's shirt!

The shortage of women at Cornell also meant that we had our pick of dates. If there had been dance cards then, all of our cards would have been full. None of the young men I met the first few weeks interested me, and when a friend of mine suggested I go out with Joe Reich—a boy I'd heard was really quite weird—I agreed. I was weird too. As one of my former high school teachers once said to me during a visit back to my school, "Dear, if we'd had the word then, you would have been a *nerd*."

Two years later, I dropped out of Cornell to marry Joe. It was not necessarily an easy decision, because I loved school, but I felt I had no other choice. My father refused to cover the cost of my education if I got married. There was no way I wasn't going to marry Joe Reich as soon as I could, and no way that Joe and I could have afforded to pay for our education ourselves. After we married and moved to California, I had a few different jobs: at a Mexican television station in San Diego, at the Pacific Telephone and Telegraph Company in Palo Alto (I lost that job when I asked to take off for the Jewish holidays!), with a nuclear physicist at Stanford—whatever would help get Joe through business school at Stanford. After our girls were born, I focused my efforts on raising them, and eventually worked as an interior designer. But through these years, I continued to crave a return to my aborted education. It's odd to think about this now, but I often looked back at a specific moment in my life that is as clear in my mind as if it happened yesterday. I was six at the time, and it was not long after the attack on Pearl Harbor. My father had been in the navy, and my family and I were on Coronado Island, near San Diego, waiting for my father's ship to arrive. Standing on the beach, I drew a circle in the sand and in that moment I understood that I could never know how many grains of sand were in that circle. This realization was followed by one that someday my parents would die, as would I. It was such a strange experience, and it wasn't until later in my life that I began to wonder how I'd learned to think in that way. I didn't know the answer, but I did know one thing: I loved learning, and I desperately wanted to return to school.

I was accepted at New York University in 1973, when Janet, our youngest, was six and I was thirty-seven. Joe fully supported my return to school, but that's not to say it didn't sometimes strain our marriage. It was eye-opening for him to discover, while I was away at class and completely unreachable, the challenges that come with parenting three girls. He figured all of it out—where the pediatrician's office was when one got sick; how quickly he could drive to their school to drop off a forgotten lunch or a note we'd forgotten to sign—and three years later, in 1976, I earned my bachelors degree. I kept going, gaining admission to the PhD program in developmental psychology at CUNY, where I first earned a master's and then, in 1986, after Debby and Marcia had graduated from college and Janet was a freshman at Stanford, my PhD. I was fifty years old at the time.

The day that I received my doctorate was a wonderful and most memorable day. Debby was living in New York, Marcia came from Boston, and Janet arrived that morning on the red-eye from San Francisco, a complete surprise that she and Joe had planned for weeks. The ceremony was at the Town Hall, and we had to arrive early to rehearse. It wasn't difficult: I was to rise from my seat, walk down the aisle, allow the dean to slip the hood—which would cover my neck and fall down my back—over my head. After this, I was to return to my seat. When the ceremony started and I rose to stand, I realized that I had a large wad of gum stuck to the bottom of one of my shoes. I did the best I could, walking awkwardly toward the stage, my right foot sticking to the floor with each step. After the dean put on my hood, two members of the psychology faculty stood and I was so sure that this wasn't really happening—that I hadn't *really* earned a doctorate—that my first thought was, *Oh no! They're standing to take it away!* But fortunately, they let me keep it and after it was all over, Joe and the girls took me to a Japanese restaurant to celebrate. We sat on the floor and the girls presented me with a large collage they had made. It had photos of me through the years under the bold headline: MOM THE DOCTOR. As I looked through the photos, I couldn't help but think of those weekend afternoons spent with my dad in the projects. I remembered how, between patients, we'd get lost in conversation, and one day, I told him that I'd decided I wanted to be a nurse when I grew up. His response surprised me: "A nurse?" he said. "I think you should become a doctor." That idea was, of course, somewhat absurd at the time. Women did not become doctors. I slid my MOM THE DOCTOR collage under my cushion and as my family toasted me, I thought of his words.

How I wished he'd been alive to see it.

———

Once we decided that we wanted to start a school, the first big question was whether it would be public or private. We considered both options. Joe had read about a philanthropist in Chicago named Joe Kellman who had recently started a free private school in an inner-city neighborhood. The Kellman Corporate Community Elementary School was the first business-sponsored elementary school in the country. Joe decided to fly to Chicago to talk to Kellman and tour the school.

"Why don't you do a private school in New York?" Kellman suggested. "Then we'll start a national chain together" We thought about it, but it didn't take long to decide that wasn't the course of action we wanted to pursue. The taxpayers of New York were already funding the public education system in the amount of about fifteen thousand dollars per child (a lot of that money, we'd come to learn, was being wasted by the so called "blob," a combination of an inefficient and oftentimes dishonest bureaucracy, unions and schools of education). Every time a child is taken out of a public school and enrolled in a private one, the system is left with the same amount of funds and fewer kids to educate, and a greater opportunity for additional waste by the blob. If we funded a private school, we as taxpayers would be paying twice to educate the kids—which was an unsustainable and unscalable idea. We decided that it made sense to start a public school, get the fifteen thousand of public dollars, spend it efficiently, and—our dream of dreams—create a model that could be replicated throughout the city.

At the time, we knew very little about public education in New York City, except that many of the zoned schools—especially those in poor neighborhoods—were abysmal and that, regardless of where they lived, it was rarely easy for families to find quality free education for their kids. When it was time for the first of our three daughters to enroll in school, Joe and I had both hoped to be able to send them to public school. After all, we were young liberals who believed in the idea of public education. We were living in Brooklyn Heights at the time, in a ground-floor rental near PS 8. Along with several other parents from the neighborhood, I went to go visit the school. It looked like a prison. There were bars on the windows, and trash in the playground. From what we heard, the classes were run with very little creativity, and the syllabus was limited and regimented. We knew this was not the place for our daughters, and we felt we had no choice but to enroll them in private schools.

That, of course, was twenty years earlier, and since then, we hadn't had any other experience with New York public schools. We had never even voted in a school board election. This was typical: less than 7 percent of New York residents have ever voted in a school-board election. We had heard of the Board of Regents—which controls the state Education Department—but in name only. We did not know its members were appointed by the Speaker of the New York State Assembly. Nor were we aware that the state Education Department was probably the most ineffectual and most overstaffed of the many bloated state agencies in Albany.

As we began to research the organization, structure, and underlying politics of public education, it became clear to both Joe and me why so many people might be as confused about the state of public education as we were. It has been rocked by great changes that started in the 1950s and has continued to lurch through seismic shifts that are very much still in motion. The first of these momentous events was the Supreme Court's 1954 Brown v. Board of Education decision, which struck down the legality of separate but equal, the doctrine that had prevailed over public education since the Plessy vs. Ferguson decision in 1896. How to apply the Brown decision has posed a problem ever since, one that has consumed time, energy, and resources with no clear effect on student achievement.

The other significant development was the unionization of public employees, specifically teachers. In 1961 the two largest teachers' unions, National Education Association (NEA) and American Federation of Teachers (AFT), had eight hundred twenty-six thousand members between them. Today, these two unions have more than four million members and, as we have come to believe after years of involvement in education, their primary mission has been to represent the interests of their members, even when those interests conflict with the needs of students. The contract for city teachers is 165 pages long, detailing things like the fact that teachers must have access to pay phones, that middle school teachers cannot be asked to teach more than three classes in a row, that no elementary school teacher has to collect milk money, and that teachers are exempt from tasks like copying school-wide documents or preparing college transcripts. The real problem, however, is that the contract has also become somewhat of a straitjacket. It prohibits the use of student results as a basis for evaluating teachers' performance, virtually guarantees lifetime tenure after three years of service, bases salary increases entirely on length of service and education courses taken, and offers a retirement plan which is so financially lucrative that it forces teachers—all of them even the good ones—into early retirement. Whereas a generation ago, teaching was one of the few professions open to women, now women represent 50 percent or more of medical, legal, and other professions. The result is that many talented people who might otherwise consider becoming teachers are now working in other fields where performance is rewarded. We've come to hold it as gospel attracting talented teachers and principals is the single most important requirement in providing a quality education, and here we were diving into a system engineered to undermine that.

In addition to these statewide issues, New York City had a whole set of problems all its own. At the time—this was in 1988—the education scene in our city was suffering from the worst effects of the failed efforts of the prior thirty years since the Brown v. Board of Education decision. The violence of the 1960s erupted in New York with Brooklyn's Ocean Hill–Brownsville riots in September 1967. This battle pitted civil rights leaders against the United Federation of Teachers (UFT) led by Albert Shanker, who grew up in Queens and taught in East Harlem in the 1950s before becoming a union organizer in 1959. Shanker made a name for himself in Ocean Hill–Brownsville in 1968, calling for a strike if fired white teachers were not reinstated. When the dust settled, New York City had created thirty-two independent community school districts controlling the education of children from kindergarten through junior high school. The members of the boards of these districts were elected. In theory this system was a good thing. However, voter turnout for these elections (perhaps because they were held in May, in isolation from other races) was extremely low. The teachers' union, with its organizing strength, was usually able to bring out just the right percentage of the vote and determine who served on these local boards. The board members in turn appointed the district superintendent, and thereby controlled who led the individual schools.

The city Board of Education, which oversaw public schools in New York City, had seven members, one appointed by each of the five borough presidents and two selected by the mayor. This made the selection of board members extremely political. Since the UFT actively donated to elected officials, its view usually prevailed when it came time to choose board members—as well as the chancellor, nominally the chief executive of the board. The position had become a revolving door for figureheads with changeovers on average every two years. Control of the first eight years of schooling was in the hands of the thirty-two independent school districts, and the chancellor's authority, such as it was, was practically limited to high schools; the structure ensured that a chancellor's job was mainly political. (This system was later reorganized by Mayor Michael Bloomberg, who won control over education in 2002 by an act of the legislature that allowed the mayor to appoint the chancellor. This authority had a sunset clause after seven years, and after another battle was renewed in 2009.)

To make matters worse, a similar power structure existed at the state level. The State Education Department was controlled by the seventeen-member Board of Regents, all of whom were appointed by the State Assembly, whose speaker was invariably a Democrat beholden to the teacher's union. The regents dictated educational policy. As a result, tenure for teachers and principals was the rule, and advancement was in no way connected to achievement. It was all a very cozy arrangement: along with the bureaucracy and the union, the educational schools formed the three-legged stool of the educational complex in the state known there as the "blob" too. Since teachers with seniority earned the right to choose where they taught, very few experienced teachers ended up in neighborhoods of poverty, which happened to be the neighborhoods where their skills were most needed.

We knew that the issue of politics would become a significant issue in our attempts to open a school, but in the early days of this work, Joe and I tried to spend less worrying about that and more on trying to figure out what type of education we needed to provide for the students that would attend our school. Our daughter Janet had become a teacher at the West Side Montessori School after studying at Stanford and NYU, and it was she who suggested the name: "Why don't you call it Beginning with Children, so everybody will always remember that this school is not about the grown-ups, but about the children in it?"

The name was perfect.

The problem, however, was that nothing like this—a public school started by private citizens—had ever been attempted before, and we had no blueprint to follow. We had specific ideas to be sure. We intended to begin operation with one kindergarten class of twenty-five students and one first-grade class of twenty-five students. The school would reflect the demographics of the community in which it was located and would be run by trustees selected from among parents, community leaders and educators. It would choose its own principal and would select students through a lottery system, picking from the parents who applied to enroll their children in the school. Our idea was that the school would be responsible to the marketplace and would include the philosophy and practices of private schools that we'd seen work: it would be run by interested community leaders who worked with parents committed to having their children attend this specific school.

After speaking to many experts in public education, including Sandra Feldman, the president of the United Federation of Teachers, we decided to build on our experiences with the Dreamers and try to open our school in District 14 in South Williamsburg, Brooklyn. We knew the great needs that existed in that community, where the zoned schools were terrible—even dangerous—and we relished the idea of providing the families there with the opportunity for a better education. We also knew that trying to open an elementary school in South Williamsburg would come with a fair share of political issues—namely, that we'd be placed in the middle of a battle between the neighborhood's Puerto Ricans, the area's largest ethnic group, and its community of Hasidic Jews. Members of this fast-growing sect of Orthodox Jews are a familiar sight in Brooklyn, looking in dress more like the eighteenth-century Eastern Europeans who started the movement than their twenty-first century Brooklynite neighbors. Rabbi Joel Teitelbaum, a holocaust survivor, lived for a time in Palestine before moving to America and founding Williamsburg's Satmar Hasidic community. This insular community thrived under the leadership of Moses Teitelbaum, Joel's nephew, from 1980 until his death in 2006. Under Moses Teitelbaum, Satmars more than doubled their ranks, to an estimated hundred thousand worldwide, building schools and expanding real estate holdings that are now worth hundreds of millions of dollars.

Despite the fact that the Hasidim made up just one-quarter of the population, they were far more politically organized than the Latinos, and they controlled the District 14 school board. The strangest part about this, perhaps, was that the Satmar held control of the school board even though their own children did not attend public schools.

We knew we'd have to walk a fine line between the two communities. To the Latinos of Williamsburg, the Satmar were the only Jewish people they knew and the Satmar's conduct produced a great deal of anti-Semitism in the Latino community we were trying to serve. Whenever we spoke, we made a point of telling the audience that we were Jewish. We also knew that we'd probably have a lot to learn about local politics. What we did not know—and never expected—was that when it came to opening our school, the biggest obstacle would not be the political tensions. Nor would it be the high rates of poverty and crime that plagued the area. Sadly, it would come in the form of our nemesis, the superintendent of School District 14, a man named William A. Rogers. Rogers, a former gym teacher, had become superintendent nearly twenty years earlier, in 1972, without ever having served as a principal. Commonly known as "'Wild Bill," he was the law in the schools of Williamsburg and neighboring Greenpoint and he ruled over his fiefdom with the kind of reckless abuse of power we would associate more with a third world dictatorship. With brusque humor, he let teachers know his initials were *W.A.R.,* and he saw to it that School District 14 name an elementary school after his hero, John Wayne, even though students were far more Latino than gringo.

We had already had several run-ins with Rogers since the onset of our "I Have A Dream" program. At that time, he was in the midst of a very public battle with the Latinos over the issue of remediation. The Hasidim wanted remediation for their children who had problems. Strangely, it was only girls who had problems. The remediation had to take place in the public schools, and the Hasidim instructed Rogers to build a wall in the schools so their children would not come into contact with the regular students. The Latino community, led by El Puente's Luis Garden Acosta, staged a major protest that was well covered in the press. When we proposed our program and it was known that it was being housed at El Puente, Rogers exploded publicly, stating that no such program would exist in his District. Through some good friends in the New York Irish community, Rogers was assured we were not bad people, and an uneasy truce ensued.

In January of 1990, Joe and I went to meet with Rogers to propose our plan to open a school. We noticed the predictable trappings: the American flag on the wall next to framed portraits of Ronald Reagan, John Wayne and Douglas McArthur. Rogers was positive and encouraging that day, and impressed that we had the support of Sandra Feldman and a number of other key players we'd met with. He offered us many suggestions about options we should pursue and people we should see. He said we should meet again. We left this first meeting encouraged by his support, and trusted that he would be true to his word and do what he could to help make a school happen.

We were wrong.

Over the next several months, and far into the next year, we continued to meet with Rogers. Joe and I had done the work: Meeting after meeting, we had presented a clear plan for what we were trying to do. We had worked out the numbers. We had developed a strong idea for a school. We had done our research to show why a different sort of school was necessary, and the types of opportunities that we wanted to bring to our students. But after every meeting, we'd leave feeling more confounded and stymied. Despite his warmth and apparent enthusiasm for what we were doing, Rogers never seemed any closer to giving us the go-ahead to open an elementary school in his district, and it was as if we were always in the same predicament: fired up to get our school opened but met with a sense of opposition and stalemating that didn't make sense to us. So many people in District 14—from Rogers to the eight members of his District 14 Board—seemed intent on pointing out why our school couldn't work, rather than why it should.

Our first and only meeting with the District 14 Board in February 1990 was downright strange. The scales dropped from our eyes that day. We arrived at District 14 headquarters at 7:00 p.m. on the nose, punctual as always. In attendance was Rogers, as well as UFT District Representative Mario DeStefano and UFT Brooklyn leader Alan Lubin, all of whom we knew. Most prominent among the board members and clearly in control were the three Hasidim: Harold Klagsbald, Isaac Brauner and Rabbi Leopold Lefkowitz.

One detail from that meeting that we always remembered later was the food. There was a lavish buffet of Italian food of which DeStefano was quite proud. He ran around teasing the Hasidim about this spread, all of which looked delicious and all of which the

Hasidim could not eat because it was not kosher. But they had come prepared: they had brought their own food along in paper bags. Clearly DeStefano had some hold over them or he would not have been joking around with them so much. One of the Hasidim, most likely the rabbi, explained to me that they could not shake my hand. I knew to wear long sleeves and dark stockings, and not extend my hand in greeting. In fact, he went on, they could not touch me at all. It did not help at all that I, too, am Jewish. Not being Orthodox, I had not been to the *mikveh* or ritual bath. I took all of this in stride and told them that of course I was familiar with their restrictions.

Rogers was strangely silent in the ensuing discussion of our plans to open a new school. Alan Lubin, the union leader, attempted to be conciliatory. The only Hasid who spoke was Klagsbald. The board agreed to appoint a committee of two of its members to work with us on the project. To us the appointment of a committee sounded good in theory. That is because we were still learning about how politicians do things: let the mind-numbing bureaucratic steps distract people and never say no, but also never do anything. This two-member committee that was allegedly created at that meeting? We never heard from any of its members—not one phone call, not one letter, not one anything. In fact, we never heard from that school board or any of its members again. But it was also at this meeting that I was coming to understand exactly what we were up against. The biggest obstacle for the bureaucrats was that this had never been done before. They didn't have a way of thinking about it and they were so committed to finding reasons to stop it, they just couldn't bring themselves to see the possibility.

# THREE

# 11 BARTLETT STREET

## *Joe*

Despite our growing frustration with the bureaucracy, Carol and I never stopped looking for a light at the end of our never-ending tunnel. That light finally appeared, two years after we began this endeavor, in May 1990, when we received an offer that was so unexpected, generous, and timely that we were sure we'd finally get the support we needed.

During my time at Reich & Tang, our firm had managed a portion of the pension funds of Pfizer, the pharmaceutical industry giant. Pfizer's CEO, Edmund T. Pratt Jr. had designated education as a company priority. To that end, the company was in the process of preparing a white paper on education and had embarked on an experiment at its research laboratories in Groton, Connecticut, which involved tapping some of its more than five hundred PhD-holding employees to teach math and science to school kids in the community. A friend at Pfizer, Kevin Keating, was familiar with our work with "I Have A Dream" in Williamsburg and told me that Pfizer still had a large physical plant in Brooklyn—in District 14, to be exact, on the border of Williamsburg and Bedford-Stuyvesant. In addition to this large manufacturing plant, the company owned several properties in the borough, including its former corporate headquarters, the original 1849 building where Pfizer was started and, as part of an area redevelopment plan, a housing project that had been underway for more than a decade and was nearing completion.

In early 1990, Kevin set up a meeting with a few of his Pfizer colleagues: Robert Schaffer, the vice president of public affairs; Donald Jacob, the vice president of external affairs; and Win Anderson, the director of corporate affairs, who was a former school principal, as well as a minister. They were enthusiastic and supportive of our idea of a school and suggested we go to Williamsburg and meet with Thomas Kline, the plant manager.

Walking around the neighborhood where the Pfizer building was located—at 11 Bartlett Street—was such a strange experience. The neighborhood had one of the highest murder rates in the city, and the poverty was palpable. It was also very apparent how divided the neighborhood was. On one hand, the streets were filled with the Hasidim, in their very traditional dress, and the women wearing wigs and long skirts. They walked the streets with Latino bodegas and abandoned buildings, their walls covered in Spanish-language posters for festivals. This was so different from where we lived. And yet, we did not feel unsafe. In all of the years that we'd end up spending here, we never felt unsafe.

When we arrived for our meeting, we entered a well maintained, fifty-year-old, four story building. Except for the top floor where there were broken windows, the building then occupied by the management of the plant was in much better condition than most of the public school buildings we had seen in New York City. We had no idea what to expect from this meeting with Tom and his colleagues, and when we first sat down at a large table in an administrative building across the street from the plant, we could not get a read on how serious they were about helping us. After we explained our intention to open the Beginning with Children elementary school and create a model for how public schools could be run, Tom smiled. He then made a big sweeping gesture with his hand, out over the table.

"We could give you this," he said.

We thought he was referring to the table at which we sat. "You want to give us the table?" Carol asked. "Thank you."

"No," Tom said. "Not the table. The whole building."

We couldn't believe it. The building was as beautiful and wonderful as anyone could imagine. We knew if it was good enough for Pfizer, it would be a wonderful school building. And with all of the new housing being developed nearby, the area was in great need of a school. This was our first lucky break in two years and, we believed, the thing we needed to actually make our school happen. After all, Pfizer was willing to donate the entire building to us at no charge whatsoever. It needed to be renovated but it was perfect for a school. How could the bureaucrats not be as hopeful and excited as we were?

———

A month later, in June, we went to Washington, DC, where the "I Have A Dream" Foundation was holding a conference. While there, we were lucky enough to be invited to the White House as part of "I Have A Dream." Among those in attendance was Joseph Fernandez, the recently appointed New York City Schools Chancellor. A week earlier, we had met with him to propose our plan and share the news about Pfizer's donation. We were honored (and a little embarrassed) when Fernandez got up to speak to the crowd and mentioned us specifically. Carol and I have never been ones for recognition, especially given the fact that the room was full of people who had all done amazing work. But after listening to Fernandez's comments—

"Joe and Carol not only brought me an idea, they brought me a building"—we realized we might have found the exact ally we'd been searching for.

Because the truth was that even after Pfizer's commitment, Rogers and his colleagues were not budging. We had taken a representative of the Board of Education to see the building, and to show him our plan: renovations on the first floor could begin immediately, and had more than enough space for kindergarten and first-grade classrooms, a dining hall, bathrooms, and a few administrative offices. During our first year of operation, we'd complete the renovations on the remainder of the building, and add extra classrooms to accommodate the additional classes we'd be adding. Pfizer had generously agreed to chip in for the costs of renovating the first floor. They had also agreed to cover the costs of heating for a set period of time, as a transition, but they wanted the Board of Education to assume them. That made sense to us. The representative from the Board of Education listened and took notes but said very little. Afterward, we didn't hear from him again.

That day at the White House, Fernandez expressed his support for what we were trying to do, and told us he would overcome any potential opposition to our plan to start our school. He'd ram approval through, if that was what it took. In the meantime, he encouraged us to continue to work with Rogers and other members of the school board.

We did our best to follow the chancellor's advice, but before long, we realized what Rogers was up to in dealing with us. He may have had a lot of swagger, but at heart he was just a bureaucrat with a bureaucrat's bag of tricks. That meant he would smile and shake hands warmly and talk a big game, but then once we were out of sight he would play the cheapest of the bureaucrat's gambits: delay, delay, delay.

I decided to be up front with him.

"The school is never going to get started, is it?" I asked him during a private meeting in his office soon after.

"No," he said.

"You're not going to be the one to stop it, either, are you?"

"Not so anybody could see that I was the one who stopped it."

"So your fingerprints won't be on that decision?"

"No."

I was appalled at his brazenness and increasingly disgusted by his unabashed willingness to say one thing in public and something else entirely in private. In fact, most of our meetings with the educational administrators in District 14 defied all standards of rationality. All the top bureaucrats at the Division of School Facilities, seemed determined to undermine us at every turn, questioning us about the number of bathrooms per floor and instructing us on rules about how big a classroom should be and how big the windows should be, and on and on, making the cost of these changes prohibitive.

We decided to go back to Joe Fernandez at the Board of Education headquarters at 110 Livingston Street. Once again, he told us that he understood the problem.

"I'm going to have to get involved directly," he said. "It's the bureaucrats again." Fernandez said he would assign someone to work with us who had direct access to him and could help us get our school moving forward. This was encouraging news, but we knew enough by this point to wait and see how his pledge of support would play out before opening the champagne. We felt we had no choice but to slow down all efforts on the school until we had someone reliable who could help us navigate the city bureaucracy and keep Fernandez involved to the degree necessary to progress.

And then we had another idea.

Our friend Jack Rosenthal had been a reporter at the *New York Times* since 1969 and had won a Pulitzer Prize eight years earlier for his work as the editorial page editor. After we called Jack and explained our predicament, he introduced us to Joseph Berger, the paper's education reporter. Berger was open to hearing our story and we invited him to come see the Pfizer building.

When Berger arrived at the plant, he introduced us to the photographer he'd brought along with him—Dith Pran, who not only was a great photographer but also a remarkable man whose story of working with Sydney Schanberg during Pol Pot's "Year Zero" murderous rampage in Cambodia was captured in *The Killing Fields*. That movie was a favorite of ours, an amazing story of courage, and just seeing Dith Pran there at the Pfizer building that day brought Carol to tears.

Joe Berger's article appeared on December 20, 1990, under the headline: "Trying to Donate a School: Generosity vs. Regulations." It detailed our efforts to open an elementary school and the resistance we were facing. Berger wrote about the fact that middle-level officials at the Board of Education believed that the Pfizer building did not meet their standards for asbestos content, for types of urinals, or for the number of windows in a room. Accepting the gift, some board officials said, would even cost the board money.

The article quoted Bill Rogers's claim that we had never returned his calls, which was almost funny it was so absurd, and summarized the bureaucrats' creative knack for creating worries and problems when they should have been seeing opportunity: Who would be responsible? Who would run the whole operation? Who were we responsible to? What children would go there? What would be the role of the chancellor's office?

Of course, we had ideas and responses to all of these questions, but none of the people we'd been meeting with during the past year of efforts ever seemed to be raising them in the hopes we might answer them.

At the time, the resistance and challenges we faced from the people whose job it was to look out for the children in their community was frustrating, dumbfounding, and more than a little heartbreaking. It just didn't make sense to us. What we didn't know at the time was that there was a massive, widespread, and ugly conspiracy underway in the district.

In 1999, years after we launched our efforts, we finally learned the truth about the rampant corruption in District 14, the tangled web of conspirators included many of the people we had met at the District Board meetings: Rogers; DeStefano, who later took over as superintendent of District 14; several members of the board; a rabbi in charge of a local religious school; and several Williamsburg housewives. The scope of the conspiracy was mind-boggling. For nearly twenty years, Rogers, and then DeStefano, created more than eighty nonexistent or no-show jobs for Hasidic housewives. In exchange, Rogers and DeStefano were guaranteed job security. The women would kick back their salaries to Rabbi Hertz Frankel, who used the funds—in the end totaling more than $4 million, to operate a private religious elementary school, Beth Rachel. The holders of these no-show jobs got to keep almost $2 million in health benefits, all without doing anything. Millions of additional dollars simply vanished. There was a second group of no-shows who worked for Beth Rachel and other United Talmudical Academy organizations and were on the board of education's payroll.

We finally understood how Wild Bill Rogers did it: he was superintendent for the unusually long period of twenty years, and this long reign was made possible by the dirty, devious Beth Rachel conspiracy that kept him in power. The operation began in the 1970s and continued up to Rogers's retirement in 1992. DeStefano, Rogers's successor, not only failed to clean up the fetid mess this scam had become by then, he in fact expanded it. District 14 stood out as having many more employees per student than any other district.

The scam was endangered as this disparity attracted more scrutiny. DeStefano came up with a shamelessly fraudulent solution: he created fictitious students, more than one thousand of them. This way he could keep the fake employees and lower the ratio. It was sickening and mercifully, a temporary fix.

Someone using the name of Concerned Citizen started sending anonymous letters about the no-shows. Somehow Rabbi Frankel got his hands on one of the letters and informed DeStefano that the jig might be up. Instead of panicking, he reclassified the no-shows, changing their paper titles from security guards to paraprofessionals. In 1994, Edward F. Stancik, special commissioner of investigation for the New York City School District, was able to obtain a search warrant to get the records from both District 14 and Beth Rachel. A five-year investigation ensued, and the conspiracy was fully revealed in 1999. The three individuals most responsible for the conspiracy— Rogers, DeStefano, and district administrator Fran Gasman—could not be held accountable since, by that time, all three had died of stomach cancer. We knew from our earlier run-ins that these were not good people, but we never imagined this level of criminality, or the tepid response the board of education would have when all of this was uncovered.

# FOUR

# TO DIE DREAMING

## CAROL

L ooking back at this period of our lives now, I sometimes can't believe we persevered. There was *always* another problem, one more issue that we couldn't see a way to resolve: The Pfizer building was located in an industrial zone, and to convert it into a school meant either changing the zoning regulations or getting a variance, a process which took months and months of meetings and money and work. Some areas of the building were full of asbestos, and nobody could seem to agree on the costs to remove it, or on a plan to do so. The bureaucrats at the Division of School Facilities continued to undermine us at every turn. After the *New York Times* article was published, we heard from people who understood how these things worked, and they all told us the same thing: you're nuts to try this! Get out now! Gene Lang advised us to stop trying to work within the school system. Frank J. Macchiarola, a former chancellor of the New York City schools under Mayor Ed Koch, suggested we give up our efforts and consider starting a private school. Ross Perot invited us down to Texas after reading the

*Times* article, and showed us the privately funded school he had successfully started there. It seemed that everyone felt we had to work outside the system.

We appreciated people's interest, and so many nights, Joe and I would discuss if perhaps they were right. Did we have it in us to continue this battle? We were both nearing our sixties; was this how we wanted to spend the rest of our lives: trapped in an agonizing hamster-on-a-wheel farce that kept playing itself out over and over again. Stuck in the same, unending conversations with the same people about zoning and board politics while nothing actually *happened*? We were being told that we could never get anywhere, no matter how well intentioned or energetic we might be, and that the best we could hope for was to make a very small splash that would count as a curiosity and little else. We'd heard that Joseph Fernandez, the schools chancellor, had been ticked off to see Joe Berger's article in the *New York Times* and was now working against us, too. It was January; we had reached another year, and still we were idling along. It was so discouraging and frustrating. We'd been at this for nearly three years, and seven months had passed since Pfizer had offered us the building. We were nearing our wits' end.

In February, it got even weirder. We sent a letter to Fernandez pointing out how ineffective the point person he had assigned to us had been. This fellow had given us a fine song and dance about how he was going to "kick ass" on our behalf—and then he did nothing. He wouldn't even answer our phone calls. Our letter to Fernandez which we faxed to him late in the afternoon produced the desired result: it was like poking a hornet's nest because a fax to the Chancellor was seen by several bureaucrats before it reached him. Within the hour we received a call from Stanley S. Litow, Fernandez's deputy chancellor. He was furious. He told me that Fernandez was more angry about this than he had ever seen him about anything. And that was the calm part of the conversation. Stan kept ranting. I tried to get him to calm down, but to no avail.

"Stan," I finally said, raising my voice ever so slightly, "if you don't stop yelling, I won't be able to hear you."

He vowed to get going and produce some results, but of course those results were going to take time, and we had to understand how tough it was to deal with the bureaucracy, and so on and so on and so on.

Looking back at the journal Joe kept at the time, I see evidence of the hopelessness we often felt. "This can never work," he wrote. "Nothing goes to closure. There is no way to work with these people. They don't take initiative. Everything falls into the abyss of *no change is possible*."

But in the end, I knew we had to keep going, because as much as the bureaucrats and politicians were getting in our way, they weren't what ultimately mattered to us. The only ones who mattered to us were the children. We were on a mission to create something that could begin to right some of the wrongs in the lives of our future students. Our opponents were fighting to preserve a crumbling status quo. We were determined to keep fighting no matter how many times they ignored us, no matter how many times they said no, no matter how many obstacles they put up. And after three decades of marriage, this surely wasn't the first time Joe and I had faced what felt to be a truly impossible goal. In fact, so many afternoons, after I'd hang up the phone with Joe, who had called to tell me of yet another roadblock, I'd think back to the years after we were first married, when we faced an uphill battle that made our efforts to start Beginning with Children feel very familiar: our struggle to start a family.

The long, oftentimes excruciating process of creating a family did not happen as I had planned it, just as the process of starting a school may not have been happening the way Joe and I had originally planned it. But I knew that despite the frustrations and gridlock we came up against time and again, it was all going to be OK, and that we could handle it. Although we were struggling mightily to start one school because we weren't just trying to start a school, we were really laying the groundwork to build a movement. We knew that something dramatically different needed to be done when it came to public education reform in New York.

The principles we were building our school on, simple and clear to us represented something potentially huge in education reform, a focus on the needs of children rather than on benefits for the involved adults. These principles—parental choice, freedom to operate in a manner consistent with the needs of specific children, parent involvement, longer school days and a longer school year, merit compensation for teachers—could be a game-changer for children of poverty. It was the growing sense of *this* possibility that re-energized us and gave us the strength to push on, for as long as necessary. Of course we would, regardless of the challenges we faced.

———

It turns out that we didn't have to wait too long. In early 1992, we got the strangest—and most wonderful—piece of news. Chancellor Fernandez had made a decision about our school. Given our long battle with Rogers and his colleagues in District 14, and their steadfast unwillingness to allow us to start a school there, the Chancellor decided that he would remove us from their purview by designating the Beginning with Children elementary school a part of the nearby high school. School districts controlled the elementary schools, but high schools fell under the authority of the chancellor. If we were designated as part of the local high school, we would no longer need the district's cooperation to open.

It was, perhaps, the most bizarre arrangement—and one that had never been tried before. Here we were, our own little school, operating a kindergarten and first-grade class as part of—at least on paper—Eastern District High School, which happened to be one of the most dangerous high schools in all of New York. Unlike every other public elementary school, we would have no relationship to our local school district. It made very little sense.

At the time—and even still today—we spent a lot of time wondering how and why this decision was made. Maybe it was because Chancellor Fernandez was afraid we would make him look bad. Maybe he came to his senses and realized that what we were proposing made a lot of sense. We'll never know, but one thing became clear to us: we wanted to start this school more than they wanted to stop us.

And we certainly weren't going to ask too many questions. All we cared about was that we were actually going to be able to open our school! The idea that we could finally devote our energies to thinking about the education of students almost felt like a luxury to us, and we wasted no time. At the beginning of March we met with our friend Lo-Yi Chan, an architect, and it was thrilling to see the physical plans take shape: the large first floor of classrooms, the space where students would eat, the office where our principal would eventually work. I was especially thrilled to see the green-shaded drawings for the empty lot near the school, which we planned to develop into a playground and garden for our students. We'd named it Charlie's Place, in honor of Charles Lubin, the founder of Sara Lee, whose daughter, Sara Lee herself a lifelong friend had offered to donate the funds for the renovation.

Noel Kriftcher, the superintendent of the Brooklyn and Staten Island High Schools (BASIS), was designated by the chancellor to chair the committee that would select the leader for our school. Noel

was a friend of Sy Fliegel and Colman Genn at the Center for Educational Innovation who supported us throughout our efforts to start
the school. Noel was not a typical bureaucrat. Rather, he had been a
successful teacher and a principal. He cared deeply about children.
His goal was the same as ours—to find the best leader for this
unusual school. Noel put Joe and me on the committee to select the
principal. This was actually a first, as usually only employees of the
Department of Education were included on such committees. Noel
also allowed us to select the parent representatives on the committee.

We held a meeting with a group of committed "I Have A Dream"
parents who volunteered to participate on the committee. We knew
it was important to have as much parental involvement in the selection process as possible, since whoever we chose as principal was
going to have a very demanding, challenging time of it and also
would be seen—rightly—as a symbol of what our vision for the
school was going to be. The meeting was held at a large conference
room at Eastern District High School, and we were pleased that it
turned out to be a high-energy gathering with a lot of good ideas
being thrown around.

It took us about two months of meetings and deliberations to
find our perfect candidate for principal: Sonia Ortiz-Gulardo. She
had spent eighteen years as an educator in East Harlem, both as a
teacher and the director of bilingual programs for the district. She
went on to direct a training program at Teachers College, Columbia
University, and then worked as the assistant director of the Mayor's
Office of Early Childhood Education, working to create a pre-kindergarten program for every four-year-old in New York City. She
was dynamite and, for years, she'd been searching for a new challenge. While it had long been her desire to become a principal, she
knew that those positions were typically doled out through political
connections—a process she had very little patience for. She'd heard

about the opening at Beginning with Children through a friend, and we invited her in for an interview. It didn't take any time at all for us to know she was our woman. When we offered her the position, she accepted immediately—having no idea what she was about to get herself into.

Sonia started in May 1992, and our plan was to open our school with fifty students in September. That meant we had four months to renovate the Pfizer building, find our students, hire our teachers, order furniture and supplies, and on and on and on. Since we were classified as part of the Eastern District High School—which already had a principal—the bureaucrats at the Department of Education decreed that Sonia had to be classified as an assistant principal. To that end, before she could begin, they made her take a test to show that she was qualified to be an assistant principal, even though she already had her principal's license. In other words, her first order of business was to prove she qualified to be demoted.

Luckily, she passed the test, and we wasted no time getting to work. Although I was still working full-time at the Lexington School for the Deaf, I managed the renovation of the Pfizer building's first floor into classrooms. When we finished that, we planned to move forward and renovate the remainder of the building. Each year, as our students progressed to the next level, we'd have to add another grade and another classroom. This meant that for the next several years, we'd always be building our school, hiring new teachers, and transforming the existing space into new classrooms.

Understanding that we'd have no school if we didn't have any children, Sonia and I began an effort to recruit potential students. We'd put a lot of thought into how we would choose the students who attended Beginning with Children, and we decided to hold an open lottery. I'd never heard of anyone doing this before, but it was the only system we could think of that would truly be fair. Sure, we could have tested children and chosen the ones who tested highest, but that wasn't what we were after. We wanted our school to be about fairness and equality, in every way possible. We wanted to create a school that gave a chance to kids who needed a chance, and a lottery seemed to be the only way to do that.

The district administrators—still unwilling to work with us— refused to grant us any access to the families at existing schools, so we had to find creative ways to reach parents and tell them about the lottery. Sonia made appointments with the directors of every day care center, and we visited places where parents with young children often went: the local McDonald's, the playgrounds, the bus stops. We got to know as many parents as we could, letting them know who we were and what we were planning.

Now, keep in mind: I'm a five-foot-tall white Jewish woman. I had, of course, spent many hours in South Williamsburg while working with our Dreamers, but most of that time was spent in the offices of El Puente. As I walked the streets of Brooklyn, I knew that I could not exactly blend into the neighborhood as much as I would have liked. But I chose not to worry about that too much. I've long believed that the way you carry yourself reflects how you're feeling on the inside, and if I carried myself as if I felt like an outsider, my idea of getting to know people—and getting people to trust me— would never work.

As a longtime New Yorker, I had come to understand one thing about New York neighborhoods: if you want to know what's happening around the streets, talk to the bodega owners. They are the eyes and ears of every community. So Sonia and I made a habit of beginning our walks around the Bartlett Street-area communities with a few stops at bodegas. We'd introduce ourselves and explain what we were trying to accomplish: creating a new school that could give the children of the community a better education and a chance at a better future.

I got to know so many wonderful people, like Mr. Rivera, who always had a fresh pot of coffee waiting for us at his bodega and wanted regular updates on our efforts. I also discovered that if I could only drink one drink for the rest of my life, it would be a *Morir Soñando*. Meaning "to die dreaming," this concoction of evaporated milk, ice, and orange juice is true to its name, and chances were, if I was walking the streets of South Williamsburg, I was doing it with a *Morir Soñando* in my hand.

During our walks, we were always armed with flyers about the school and the lottery, which we kept stuffed in a large shoulder bag decorated with images of Kermit the Frog. (For some reason, I have always adored that little green guy.) Mr. Rivera and the other bodega owners always happily tacked our flyers to their wall. When it came time for us to hold open houses where parents could come in and learn more about the school, he would send over coffee and rolls. Not once would we be charged for these items.

Because the school was under construction, we held these open houses in a large conference room at the Pfizer building across the street from the school, and we'd spend the evening answering questions and talking more about the type of school that Beginning with Children would be: an environment with high academic standards that encouraged family and community involvement. In many ways, we were out to create a liberal arts education, beginning in kindergarten. It would be academically well rounded, with classes in music and art, and a focus on exposing students to the world around them. It would be child-centered, where students would, we hoped, be excited to learn; where they could learn *how to* learn. In many ways, it would be similar to the education I received at the Lab School.

Of course, we couldn't provide all of the programs we wanted with the money the city was able to commit to the school, so Joe and I decided to start the Beginning with Children Foundation as a way of bringing additional funding to the school. We contributed

$500,000 of our money, and Pfizer committed another $500,000. Not only would that money go toward renovating the first floor, it would also fund the creation of art and music programs which had been a casualty of the 1970's budget crunch. With additional help from the Equitable Foundation, we were planning to build a science lab—a lively, engaging environment in which our students could experience a hands-on approach to science. Science for lower school children was another casualty of the 1970's crunch.

When we spoke of these plans, parents would look at us with excitement and hope, and then with confusion. "And this is a public school?" we'd hear again and again, their voices steeped in skepticism.

"Yes," we'd say.

"And it's *free?*"

After one open house, several parents asked if they could come back and tour the building. Now, remember: It hadn't been used for ten years. Pigeons still lived on the fourth floor. There were construction workers everywhere, and dust up to your ankles. Walls were either in the process of being knocked down or built up. I looked at Sonia.

"What should we do?" I asked her in a whisper.

"We should order a whole bunch of hard hats. And hope they don't run."

It took a lot of imagination to see the building as a future school, and most of our parents walked around in a daze.

"You mean to tell me this will be my child's classroom two months from now?" one woman yelled to us over the noise of a man jackhammering nearby.

In the end, we received exactly 50 applications for fifty slots—twenty-five kindergarteners and twenty-five first-graders, and, since that was exactly how many spots we had open, we were thrilled that we could accept them all. Sonia and I will always remember that first group of parents as very special people. They took a leap of faith with us, knowing that we were trying to accomplish something that had never been attempted and and having no idea if we could actually pull it off. And I'd say the same thing about the teachers we hired, and the secretaries who came onboard, and even the bodega owners, who all worked together to make the school happen. Because in that setting in South Williamsburg, it was people like these men and women, with their cold *Morir Soñandos,* their hot coffee, their warm inviting smiles, and their belief that if we could dream it we could do it, who instilled in me the belief that it had, of course, been worth it to keep fighting.

———

Our school was scheduled to officially open on September 24, 1992. The day before, we had a party to dedicate the school. Having once believed that this day would never come, neither Joe nor I slept very much the night before. Under large white tents in the back of 11 Bartlett Street, hundreds of people gathered to help us celebrate the beginning of Beginning with Children. Everyone we loved was there, along with people from Pfizer, elected officials, Gene Lang, Mr. Rivera, and most important of all, our children and their parents. There were face-painters and balloons and different activities for the kids to enjoy. We served hot dogs and hamburgers, alongside empanadas and cake from the local Latino bakery.

Tom Kline, whose initial generosity (along with the generosity of so many others), had made this day possible, gave a moving speech under one of the tents against a backdrop of blue, green, and yellow balloons.

"I'm sure that the record will say in the year 2135 that this school has graduated hundreds upon hundreds of caring, sharing, educated individuals who will have given back much of what they have learned to the needy of their community," Tom said.

The next day was the first day of school. Unfortunately (and maddeningly), 11 Bartlett Street was not quite ready for the students, so, in order to keep our opening date, we decided to begin classes in one double-size room at Eastern District High. I was worried sick about having to break this news to our parents, and I was convinced that none of them would agree to send their kids to the school that had one of the highest murder rates in the city. But the parents surprised us. Not one of them refused to send their kids over to Eastern District High.

We had taken the precaution of hiring special security guards for our classes, but in the end, that didn't seem necessary. Many high school students took it upon themselves to accompany and protect our kids when they had to move through the building. These were pretty tough kids, doing the guarding. And when it came time for us to move, after a month, these kids volunteered to help us move into our own building.

Those first weeks were so frantic we could hardly believe it when, on February 25, we reached our hundredth day of being in operation. To celebrate, the kindergarten class brought in one hundred jelly beans and one hundred pieces of popcorn. Zoraida Olivo, the school secretary, baked a cake in the shape of "100" to mark the occasion. One of the students, a boy named Kendall*, held the kindergarten door open, shook the hand of each visitor and said, "Thank you for coming to my school."

Not long after, Cornell University invited me to campus to talk about our experience opening a public school in Brooklyn. I was honored to be invited, and touched that more than one hundred people showed up to hear me speak. After I finished, and the room had mostly cleared out, a young woman came up and introduced herself to me.

"I'm an activist," she told me. "I've always thought you had to carry placards and protest outside to get things done. But you've done it from the inside. What an inspired idea that was."

As I drove home the next morning, I thought about our students who were just arriving in their classrooms to start the day, and remembered that day, four years earlier, when Joe had first proposed the seemingly crazy plan that we try to open a school.

*Yes,* I thought. *What an inspired idea it was.*

# PART
# 2

# FIVE

# DOING SOMETHING
# (EVEN IF WE DID IT WRONG)

*CAROL*

When Joe was a high school student in Charleston, West Virginia, he worked part-time after school and on Saturdays at a butcher shop called the Sanitary Meat Market. The manager hired Joe for eighty cents an hour, aware that this young man, just fifteen years old, knew very little about being a butcher. For the first few days at that job, Joe stood behind the counter, feeling lost and useless, until one day a butcher named Clyde Legg, whom everyone called Junior, marched over to Joe, put his face, reeking of moonshine, near Joe's and barked, "Do something, even if you do it wrong!"

Junior's advice to Joe became our mantra during the early days of Beginning with Children. Since neither Joe nor I—or even Sonia, for that matter—had experience starting a school from the ground up, we often had no idea what we were doing. But we decided that the only way forward was to keep going: to do *something*, even if we did it wrong. It wasn't a bad strategy;—it kept us moving forward, and later, whenever we saw articles in which people were asked to credit the teacher or mentor most responsible for their success, we chuckled and remembered Junior—uneducated, rarely sober, but very wise.

As we came to learn—the hard way—new public schools don't get built that frequently, and those that do are part of a large machine. Our school was different. Because we didn't have the support of the local school board, it often felt like we were operating in total isolation, left to our own devices. We had so much to figure out: the bus service and bus routes, how lunch would be served, where to send the payroll, where to order supplies. During the first few weeks, we'd get calls from a parent whose child was dropped off at the wrong bus stop, miles from his house. We'd have days when lunches—which were packaged and delivered from Eastern District High School—never arrived. But everyone always pitched in to help. If a child needed to get picked up, we'd pick him up. If the lunches didn't arrive, Sonia and our two wonderful secretaries, Gladys Guadalupe and Zoraida Olivo, would run to the local grocery store and bring back as much peanut butter, jelly, and bread as they could carry. Betty Cotes, a teacher's assistant, would join them in the dining room and they'd work as quickly as they could to make fifty sandwiches. We got to know our bus drivers, and even our local police and firemen. And it quickly became clear to us: the more that people in the community began to understand what we were doing—that the school we were running was special—the more people chipped in to help us out.

One of my favorite quotes is one by our friend Wendy Kopp, the founder and CEO of Teach For America. In her book *One Day, All Children*, she states, "That educational equality is possible gives us the responsibility—and the opportunity—to make it happen."

It was only after our school opened that we truly began to understand what educational equality meant. Walking into Beginning with Children, you knew that you were not in a typical school. Because we wanted our school to not only be special but to *feel* special, we put thought into every last detail, even the way that the rooms and hallways looked. While we had been told that standard regulations for elementary schools included painting the walls either a mustard yellow or a dull gray, we chose to simply ignore those rules. We painted our walls a bright white and covered the floors in sky blue tiles. Instead of the long, industrial tables that you typically find in a lunchroom, we chose round tables that seated ten. These fostered conversation and a teaching atmosphere. There were comfortable couches in a nook on the second floor, and plants dangled in front of every window. We even had a staffed nursery where teachers could drop off their children, at no charge. We thought this was a wonderful idea, and our teachers with children truly appreciated the opportunity to spend time with their children during the work day. Not long after we started operations, Carol Gresser, the president of the Board of Education, came to visit our school. She walked around our classrooms and halls in amazement.

"How did you get to use these paint colors and choose these types of tables?" she asked us.

"We just did it," I explained, a little nervous that we'd been found out, and that there'd be trouble.

"Well, keep doing it," she whispered, advising us that ignoring the Board of Education's rules would be fine as long as we stayed under the radar. We took that as a sign that what we were doing was working. And to be honest, we knew that despite the challenges we faced and our lack of experience, we really were succeeding in our desire to create a school where everyone—students and teachers and parents alike—felt both valued and empowered. You'd see it in the students: Boys like Omar Lopez, who arrived at school every day in a pair of shorts and a bow tie and who Sonia thought of as our school's first Dominican mayor. Or beautiful little Julio*, who didn't have his front teeth until he was in the fourth grade. His first great love was gymnastics. As Sonia and I worked in the office, we'd often hear a *plump, plump, bump* down the hall. It was Julio doing cart-wheels and somersaults, and every time he was caught, he'd simply smile and take a bow.

A lot of our success was thanks to the wonderful teachers we'd been so fortunate to find—and who had taken a chance on us—and to Sonia, who was an impressive leader and a very effective principal. She understood what teachers needed, and she knew how to support them. She gave them the freedom to make choices, within clearly stated guidelines, about what and how they taught. Because we did not report to the school board and were largely left on our own, we had the space to let our teachers be innovative and creative in their work. They were—and they were also like a family to each other. Teachers often met in private to discuss different students, to figure out if they could collectively understand why a certain child was struggling, and what strategies could help another child learn. At the time, I often thought back to an experience I had had years ear-lier, while in graduate school and working at Bank Street College, a New York City school, that operated according to the philosophy of John Dewey. For my PhD, I studied deaf infants, and my work at Bank Street helped pilot test the use of closed-captioning in educa-tion. One day, I was observing a class of deaf students who were watching a video about nursing whales. A student stopped the lesson and asked: Because whales are mammals, they must nurse their young, but since they live in the ocean, how does the mother whale share her milk with her young? Doesn't the milk get lost in the ocean water?

This was a very good question, and none of the adults in the room, myself included, had the answer. In some schools, the teacher may have felt compelled to make up an answer, but this teacher ad-mitted the truth: she had no idea. It was powerful, witnessing this type of relationship between a teacher and her student, where the teacher could admit to her own limitations. When the day ended, I decided to call a scientist I knew and ask him if he could answer this student's question, but I have to admit, I was a little afraid of where this information might lead. I wasn't sure that I wanted to get into a discussion—using my somewhat rudimentary sign language, no less—about the nursing, and perhaps sexual, habits of whales. When I returned to the school with an answer, the student was far less interested in what I had found out than he was in *how* I had found out.

"Well, I asked someone who knew. Because I didn't."

"I guess we all learned something, then," the student responded.

*That* was the sort of teaching environment we were out to create at Beginning with Children—a place of true learning—and I visited the school nearly every day to keep track of our progress. I always tried to get there in time for the morning ritual: as students arrived, Sonia would personally greet them at the entrance. Afterward, the students would gather on large, colorful rugs in their classroom and Sonia and I would remind them that here at school, they were valued and respected. We ended each morning by reminding them that they could become *anything* they wanted to be: if they could dream it, they could do it.

"Can we be you?" students would often ask Sonia, me, or one of the teachers.

"Of course! You can become that and so much more!"

———

Just as we didn't realize how involved we would eventually become with our Dreamers, we also didn't anticipate getting to know our students as well as we did during those first few years. Our youngest grandson, Asher, recently explained it more clearly than I ever could. He dropped out of prekindergarten twice. (It's a family tradition—I flunked it once.) Afterward, he didn't want to go to school. When we asked him why, he said, "I'm worried that if I get sad, nobody will know I'm sad, and there won't be anyone to talk to." (He's fine now.)

But our school wasn't like that. If Asher was sad, people would know he was sad, and they'd certainly ask him about it. One morning, I arrived at the school to find that a student had a black-and-blue outline of a handprint on his cheek. I was so mad I could barely concentrate that day. A week later it was parent-teacher night, and when the father of that student arrived, I was very clear with him: we saw that bruise, and we don't ever want to see it again. It didn't go as well as I'd planned. The man grew very angry, and he came at me swinging. Caught off guard, I grabbed on to his extended arm. When Joe walked into the room right then, I was swinging from this man's arm like a Flying Wallenda. It was not an approach I'd recommend, but I will say that we never saw another mark on that child's body.

The interest in our students even went beyond the administrators and teachers. We were lucky to be assigned a wonderfully kind man named Hector as our custodian. He kept an eye on all of the kids, and if they were having a bad day, he'd go out of his way to find out why. One of our students, a first grader named Carl*, was a great kid, but he had a lot of discipline problems and he often got upset during the school day. To be honest, this was not unusual for our students. What we eventually came to realize is that our school attracted many children who struggled at the zoned school—kids who didn't quite fit in there, or who had behavioral issues. At that school, the staff of teachers and administrators was overworked, or simply unmotivated, and these kids often got lost. When our school opened, a lot of parents saw it as an alternative that might help their struggling child. We were open to educating every single child who wanted to come to our school, but some students—like Carl, for instance—required a bit more attention. Whenever Carl would get upset or misbehave, Hector would come to Sonia. "I see Carl is having a rough day," he'd say. "Mind if I put him to work in the dining room?" For a half hour, Carl would stand beside Hector, helping him sweep or wipe down the tables. In between their work, they'd talk. Before long, Carl would be calm enough to return to class.

We had never truly doubted that our efforts to fight for higher standards in our school would lead to this sort of environment, but it was wonderful to see we were right. I remember when we finally realized that we might have done what we set out to accomplish, during the third year that our school was in operation. I loved spending time in the library, an airy, spacious room we'd built on the fourth floor, where the pigeons had once lived. Thanks to a generous donation from the Robin Hood Foundation, it had become a place that was filled not just with books, but with a palpable love of reading. The teachers had organized a poetry contest, and the winning poems were printed on the window shades, along with inspirational quotes from famous writers and artists, so that when the kids looked up from their books and out the windows, they saw poetry instead of poverty. One such quote was from Groucho Marx: "Outside of a dog, a book is a boy's best friend. Inside of a dog, it is too dark to read."

One day, I took a seat on a low table in the hall to wait for Berkys to finish in the classroom. "Carol, don't you know that sitting on tables is not allowed?" a third-grader named Sidney* inquired before politely asking me to move.

I did as I was asked, of course, and Sidney then suggested that, while I waited, he might read to me. He read beautifully from a book he seemed to know by heart. I'd had experience before with children who had memorized a book without actually being able to read what was on the page. I wanted to be sure. So I thanked Sidney and asked if he would read one more book to me.

"Carol, do you want me to choose one by the same author and illustrator?" he asked.

"Yes, please!" I said.

Sidney walked off to explore the library shelves and was soon back reading to me. I had to hold back my tears in that moment. It had always been our idea that by trying to do things differently—to do the best we could for our students—we'd be able to create experiences just like this for students such as Sidney.

This thinking also applied to the things we expected from our students' parents. In fact, our philosophy on parental involvement was wildly at odds with New York City public school tradition from the outset. Many schools had a yellow line painted on the street outside the school that parents were forbidden to cross. The rules were clear. Parents were *not* to cross that line. They were *not* to enter the building. Our parents were accustomed to being invited to their child's school for one reason: their son or daughter had gotten into trouble. We took the opposite approach. When parents first applied to enter the lottery, we explained that they, too, were required to participate in the life of the school. They could choose the manner in which they were involved—helping to serve lunch, assisting in a classroom—but it was a requirement we were going to insist on. Other schools worried about how to keep parents out. We worried about how to keep the parents in. We wanted them around as much as we could get them. So we spent a lot of time thinking about how to involve the parents as much as we could, to make the school more than just a school—to make it a central force in the community. That was how we came up with notion of a parent room: a place where parents would *always* feel welcome. We went to the Department of Education and requested permission to install several free washers and dryers in the family room. I loved the idea and imagined how lively a room it would eventually become—filled with our students' parents, who'd come not just to do their laundry but to better get to know their child's teachers and, best of all, each other. We were heartbroken to be told that, due to liability issues, the Board of Education was denying our request. It wasn't our first choice, but we renamed the lunch room that was already in place the family room. On the walls, we eventually hung a framed photographic portrait of each of our students, just like we'd hung dozens of photos of our children and grandchildren in our living room at home, and we let the parents know that they were always welcome to visit.

We'd often hear stories from our friends at the bodegas about how pleased our parents were not only with the education their children were receiving, but for the way they themselves were being treated. We got a sense of this on the night of our first parent-teacher conference. We decided that we wanted to do a little something extra. The parents had put their faith in us, and that had always meant a lot to us. At the time, Joe was the chairman of a photography company, PCA International, Inc., which employed a group of traveling photographers who took millions of school pictures every year. We decided to have a PCA photographer come out to Beginning with Children and take pictures of the kids and their families—and we meant entire families, including the dog and, even on a few occasions, the goldfish. On the night of the parent-teacher conferences, we gave each family a box of their photos.

"I can't believe you're giving this to me," one mother said with appreciation when the evening had ended. "What a nice gift."

I took her hand. "I can't believe you've given us your child, and made the choice to believe in us. There's no better gift than that for us."

# SIX

# LESSONS LEARNED

## *JOE*

O f course, all of this is not to say that everything went smoothly during our first few years of operation. Our goal was to begin with one kindergarten and one first-grade class and build the school to the sixth grade, adding two classes of twenty-five students each year. This meant that we were always in the process of expanding—renovating the upper floors into additional classrooms, finding new young students to replace those that were progressing to the next class, hiring new teachers. When we first opened the school, we weren't sure that we'd get the money to complete the expansion. We had renovated the first floor for $1 million—half of which we had donated, and the other half of which had come from Pfizer. The staff at the Board of Education had estimated that we could renovate the remainder of the building for an additional $2 million, which was the amount they could provide under their capital plan. We knew that number was a fantasy and that we'd need closer to $5 million, but we held our tongues and opted not to contradict the staff recommendation. We figured it would be even harder to close a school than it had been to open one. And who knew? Maybe the additional funds would magically appear somehow.

Soon after classes started at 11 Bartlett Street, we got a call from Pfizer's Tom Kline, who told us we were about to be summoned to Borough Hall, the headquarters of the borough president. Tom's manner, although mysterious, suggested that this was good news, so we arrived at the office of Brooklyn Borough President Howard Golden feeling hopeful. And we were justified in doing so: Golden told us he had awarded us an additional $2.75 million from funds he controlled to complete the construction of the school. I think it took my wife about five seconds from the time she heard this piece of great news to get to work managing the renovation. In fact, she was so adept as a construction manager I nearly expected her to come home in the evening dressed in a hard hat, overalls, and work boots.

Herbert Construction was the company the School Construction Authority selected to perform the renovations. A few days after we heard this news, we received an invitation to breakfast at the Brasserie with Anthony Scotto, who was the Herbert Construction marketing representative who would be working on our job. We arrived at the Brasserie and were met by Anthony, a handsome, well-dressed man. We sat down at our table and all of a sudden his suit pocket began to vibrate and ring. It was his cell phone—a device we'd never seen before! Although this was 1993, long before the days of the internet and the investigative power of Google, Anthony clearly had done his homework on us. He seemed to know every detail of our personal and professional history. We soon learned that his history was much more interesting! Over breakfast, he explained that he had previously been in another field until "the government had forced a career change" on him. His wife, Marion, served as the unpaid special assistant to Borough President Golden.

Over breakfast, Anthony told us he was our man at Herbert and if any problems came up, we should not hesitate to contact him directly. Carol followed his advice to the letter. Any time she was being ripped off by a subcontractor or had any other issue, she would put in a call to Anthony, and he would solve the problem. We remain friends with the Scottos to this day and are frequent clients of their restaurant, Fresco by Scotto, where we are always greeted with warmth.

Fortunately for us, the man who was the head of the construction crew at Beginning with Children had once been a teacher himself, and he worked hard to make sure the work happened as quietly as possible while classes were in progress during the school day. He often did even more for the children, in fact—buying ices for the kids when the weather turned warm, and hosting a BBQ for them on the last day of the school year.

One of the problems we confronted during the renovation was something we never could have planned for. Unbeknownst to us, there were things called labor coalitions operating throughout the city. They had been mostly minority run and dated back to the 1960s, when they were founded as a means to combat racial discrimination on job sites. Many of these coalitions had lost their way since then, sadly, and had become populated by criminals who would show up at construction sites, claim there were not enough minorities on the job, and then use fierce intimidation tactics, and even violence, to talk their way into a job. A few years earlier, thirty-one members of labor coalitions had been indicted on extortion charges, and the boss of one coalition had pleaded guilty to grand larceny. After our renovations began, it became clear that our school was a target. On many days, vans would pull up in front of our school, packed with at least fifty men, many of them carrying baseball bats and sawed-off lead pipes. They would accuse us of not having enough minorities among the crew and demand to be hired on the spot. One morning, when these men were told that their help wasn't required, they tried to push their way into the school, when only

Carol and Sonia were there to stop them. Sonia called the police, who quelled the situation, but the men were back two days later. They eventually stopped coming, and we later learned that they had been paid off to stay away from the school. By whom, we never knew.

We also had a lot to learn, and never could truly escape from the frustrations of working within such a huge, mismanaged bureaucracy. Take, for example, the free nursery we had set up for our teachers. We had taken the legal precaution of having the teachers who used the nursery sign a release form, protecting the school if a child was injured while on site. Every teacher in our school who was a mother was more than happy to sign it in exchange for free child care just steps from their classroom. We quickly understood that should this arrangement be adopted on a system-wide basis throughout the educational system in New York, it would materially reduce the attrition problem that cost the system many young and talented teachers each year. However, before long, the Board of Education got wind of what we were doing. Our nursery was declared illegal and we were forced to close it down.

The same went for the free classes we set up for parents of our students. After conducting a survey of some of the parents in our school, we discovered that many of them wished for an educational experience of their own—instruction on the use of computers and classes on child development. We decided to address their concerns and established free classes on child development, which Carol developed and taught. The classes were a huge hit, with nearly 90 percent of all parents participating at some point. Yet a union representative who'd heard what we were doing called to tell us that she was prepared to file a grievance against the school unless we discontinued the courses. The problem? Carol was not a "licensed" teacher. Yes, she had been president of a school for eight years and held a PhD in developmental psychology, but the union didn't care about that. Carol agreed to stop teaching the classes, and we ended up having to reestablish them with a certified teacher, at far greater expense and with much reduced attendance.

We also ran into quite a bit of difficulties because we were considered part of the high school division. As such, our students were in the database of high school students, which meant they got the mailings sent to these students. It just so happens that one of these mailings involved information on practicing safe sex. Included in the mailing were a few free condoms.

"Are you expecting me to hold on to this for the next decade or so, or do you have another idea?" one parent asked, understandably angry, when her five-year-old son received his condoms in the mail.

It was a disaster, the typical result of decisions made miles away, and we were relieved and excited when, during our third year of operation, we got word that Ramon Cortines, who replaced Joseph Fernandez as schools chancellor, had decided to take Beginning with Children out of the high school division. In 1994, he placed a resolution before the Board of Education that designated us as a school. We even got a number, PS 333, which we never used. Because we were to become the first elementary school to *not* be part of a district, we expected opposition to the resolution from the districts. Strangely, the resolution passed without discussion.

Becoming our own school was good news, but there were some initial hurdles to cross. For example, we once again had to go through the process of figuring out a myriad of administrative issues: where to send payroll, where to order supplies. Since we were the only elementary school reporting to the Board of Education, we were like a freestanding entity. We, in effect, had no supervisor and were free of much of the bureaucracy. The reorganization also meant that we were now entitled to have a principal rather than an assistant principal. Of course, Sonia *had* been our principal, regardless of the title she'd held, and there was no question in our minds that she would continue to be our principal. Even so, the Board of Education required us to open the position to a citywide search. By this time, the school had gotten some publicity and we received many applications. This meant that Sonia had to spend weeks giving tours of the school to the applicants applying for her job, which she had no intention of leaving. And this time, there was no Noel Kriftcher to guide us. The process was "managed" by Board of Education bureaucrats at the infamous 110 Livingston Street. Where originally we had completed the three-phase hiring process in two months, this time around it took the full twelve months allowable under the law. We got the final signature approving Sonia as the principal just one hour before the one-year mark was about to expire, and thank heavens, or we would have had to start all over again!

―――――――

As exasperating as these little annoyances could be, we found they meant very little compared to the biggest challenge of operating a public school in one of the most disadvantaged parts of the city: the realities of living in poverty, faced every day by our students and families.

Nearly all of our students were very poor, at or below poverty, and many of them were new to the United States, having immigrated from countries where children still worked long hours in the fields, and where it was expected that children would take care of their parents in old age. That was a system that made every bit of sense in the absence of luxuries like social security or health insurance, but it was not a system that necessarily translated well to life in the United States.

Here we came, offering what we thought were the kind of opportunities all parents would want. But our offer had more ramifications than we understood at the time. The opportunities we offered also carried the potential to loosen those vital connections between our students and their parents. The parents might even view those opportunities as something that would take their children away from them and deny them the secure future they had always expected. Only very gradually, incident by incident, did we even begin to understand these complexities.

One particularly jarring learning experience came when we organized a trip for our first sixth-grade class to Cornell University, our alma mater. We wanted our students to see firsthand just what possibilities awaited them if they worked hard and made it through school. The university agreed to host us, and we eagerly loaded the group of teachers, parents, and students onto two buses for the drive up to Ithaca, New York. We arrived at Cornell, with its beautiful, bucolic quads and its ivy-covered stone buildings, excited for our students and their families. As we walked across the campus to where the university had reserved real dorm rooms for us to stay, we knew that nobody in the group had ever been in such a setting before.

For the next day, we had organized a tour of campus. During this tour, we noticed that some of the parents looked uncomfortable. Others seemed downright angry.

Carol and I approached one woman and asked if everything was OK. It was not. "How can you do this?" she asked us in an agitated whisper. "How can you take our kids to see all of this when they can never have it?"

We were shocked. She went on to explain that this place seemed like Disneyland to her, a fairyland where real people had no place. She almost went so far as to call Carol and me misguided do-gooders who were taunting them with visions of the impossible.

"But your child can have this," Carol told her. "That is why we are here! We will show them and you that they can have it."

But that woman, and many of the other parents, couldn't see it. They couldn't see it then, and they couldn't see it even after a presentation from students who attended the university on full scholarship, who explained all of the options granted by financial aid.

The bus ride back to New York was quiet, and Carol and I felt crestfallen. What we did not realize then, and not for a long time afterward, was that the anger these parents felt went much deeper than the question of what would be possible for their kids. For the parents it was as if they themselves were being—at worst—taunted or—at best—reminded of all the opportunities they had themselves been denied. Their lives had been shaped by a deep, slow burn at being excluded from such magical chances at making better lives for themselves. Back home after the trip, Carol reminded me of the conversation we'd overheard nearly ten years earlier, when a woman from JHS 50 had called our Dreamers "garbage." The fallout from some adults at Cornell had helped her understand, at least a little, why someone would say that. When you've been denied opportunities for so long, it might be difficult to see others—even your own children get the chances you were denied.

And what was more, despite the world we created inside our school, none of us could escape the reality playing out on the other side of the wall. In fact, the normal routine at the school was staged against the backdrop of violence. We experienced the very worst of this at the end of our first year. We'd planned to hold a celebration picnic at Charlie's Place, the playground and garden we had developed on land nearby. Everyone was looking forward to the picnic, but that morning, as we readied the students to go, we received news that a twelve-year-old had just been murdered in front of the high school across the street from Charlie's Place. We quickly canceled the picnic and kept the students inside the school. That day, as the police investigated this murder, they found the body of a young woman, another murder victim, lying in the grass of an empty lot near the school. The following day, another teenager—this one a sixteen-year-old boy—was murdered in front of the same high school. Many of our kids witnessed that murder, and FBI agents and police cars filled the street in front of our school.

In the journal Carol kept, she labeled this whole section "Carnage." In it, she wrote with a sense of hopelessness that still makes my heart ache. But even this terrible stretch of days would not compare to the day two years later when one of our own students in our newly opened prekindergarten—a sweet, quiet four-year-old named Tony*—was murdered alongside his mother by her drug-crazed lover. We held a memorial service at Beginning with Children, and it was among the most devastating experiences of our lives. We were in our early sixties at this time and had never experienced that kind of loss directly. Yet we knew that so many people who came to the service had attended many similar services already, following the murder of a child, or the death of a relative at the hands of a family member, or in the name of drugs. After Tony's service ended, Carol and I went home and talked at length about what to do. We'd been naive, we realized, to hope that the school alone could rapidly turn around the neighborhood and give the community a greater sense of hope.

A few days later, the school year came to an end. Carol and I were both there to see the students off and wish them well. The children were all sitting at their desks, in their bright classrooms, and when the final bell rang, many of them lingered. Some refused to leave, and went to sit in their cubbies—a wooden closet where they would hang their jackets and bags. When we asked them why, we heard the same answer again and again: they felt safe at school. This was something we also heard from parents about the school.

We allowed the children to stay for an hour or so and then gently ushered them home so that our teachers could prepare to go home themselves. As we stood at the school's entrance and bid them good-bye, I thought to myself: we are doing all we can to help these students. We had reached our goal of opening one school, and we knew that we'd accomplished all that we could. This was all we could do.

Or was it?

# SEVEN

# A NEW WAY FORWARD: CHARTER SCHOOLS

## CAROL

I f either of us had ever heard of the idea of a charter school during our early years working in South Williamsburg, neither of us remembers. The first time we can recall being aware of the notion was when the co-executive director of the Robin Hood Foundation, Norman Atkins, told us he was leaving Robin Hood to start a charter school across the Hudson River in Newark, New Jersey.

At the time, we hadn't the foggiest idea what that meant.

To fully grasp the roots of charter schools, one has to go as far back as 1215, the year the famed Magna Carta was issued in England as a fiery statement on behalf of liberty and in favor of limitations of the English monarchy's power. This so-called Great Charter stood for centuries as the most notable example of a charter—that is, a document granting authority under certain conditions.

A Massachusetts education professor named Ray Budde, who had taught seventh grade and served as an assistant principal, is largely given credit as the person who first turned the concept of charters toward education. In 1988, he published *Education by Charter: Restructuring School*

*Districts.* In it, he evoked the example of the Magna Carta and other famous charters, such as that granted to explorer Henry Hudson by the East India Company, in pressing educators to make structural changes to encourage innovation and fresh thinking.

Budde suggested that groups of teachers be given contracts, or "charters," by their local school boards to explore new approaches. He argued that given the rapid social change in the United States there was a need for this type of experimentation. A charter, he argued, was a useful instrument that could be applied to our contemporary education system, and used to create a local authority with powers different from what currently existed. "For a charter to be approved," he wrote, "it would have to contain a predetermined program evaluation plan which involved genuine outside participation."

Budde's idea that charter schools could acquire varying degrees of autonomy in exchange for stricter accountability was embraced by education reformers across the nation, and the idea of what, exactly, a charter school could be was shaped. In short, a charter school is an independently run public school granted greater flexibility in its operations, in return for greater accountability for performance. It does not operate under the direct jurisdiction of a school board, but under the specific provisions of a five-year charter granted by the state. That means that charter schools, which exist as distinct legal entities, are not subject to all the same rules and regulations as a typical public school. Although they are public schools financed by public funds, they are governed by their own specific charter rather than by the existing public school regulations. This autonomy allows the school to set the length of the school day and school year; create its own curriculum; select, evaluate, and compensate its staff; and allocate the dollars awarded to the school by the state in the way that the school— and not the bureaucracy—deems best. Students are assigned to a charter school based on lottery results rather than on where they lived. And, most important, unlike traditional public schools—

which are almost never closed, however poor their performance—charter schools may be shuttered if they fail to meet the terms of their charter.

Albert Shanker, then president of the American Federation of Teachers, read Budde's book the year it came out. Soon after, he gave a speech endorsing Budde's ideas at a conference on improving public education in Minnesota, a speech that partly led to that state becoming the first in the nation to pass a charter school law in 1991. In future speeches and articles, Shanker suggested that small groups of teachers and parents submit proposals to a panel consisting of local school board officials, who could then issue charters for a period of years. Shanker did allow that rules could be bent if 65 percent of teachers, the principal, the union representative, and the superintendent all agreed to change them. But he was definitely advocating a teacher-led vision for charter schools.

This was the extent of our understanding of charter schools when we took Norman Atkins up on his offer and attended an event at his charter school, North Star Academy, in Newark, New Jersey, early in 1998, its first year of operation. It was truly inspirational. The staff was young and enthusiastic, and they beamed when the students arrived in their crisp uniforms and declared their commitment to learning. The board members we met seemed fully committed to the success of the school, the most memorable being Cory Booker, who at the time was a young recent graduate of Stanford University but who would go on to become Newark's mayor. We learned that the children had all been selected by lottery and that the New Jersey charter law allowed the school to be independent of Newark's failing public school system. The principal and board members stood and spoke of their desire to serve their students by building an uncommon school where students would participate in a rigorous, ten-month, extended-day academic program designed to help them excel in school and life. They spoke of the work they'd undertaken to shape an intimate, supportive, engaging school community where classes were small and personalized; where parents were partners; where teachers taught with passion and commitment; and where all the adults modeled—and all the students developed and lived—the values of caring, respect, honesty, justice, and self-discipline.

At the end of the ceremony, a board member approached Joe and me. We could see the pride on his face. After we congratulated him, he asked us an interesting question.

"Think something like this could ever happen in New York City?"

Joe and I just looked at each other. Although neither of us said it out loud, I knew what we were both thinking: it already had.

———

From the moment we learned about charters, we were onboard. Since the beginning, our goal for Beginning with Children was to create a public school that could serve as a model for the reform of public education—to show the type of success that is possible when children are taught they can learn and achieve, when teachers and administrators are empowered to do their job, and when parents and the surrounding community become involved in the educational experiences of the children. These principles were at the center of charter schools, and we felt so excited about the possibilities a New York charter law could bring to students not only in South Williamsburg, but across our city and state. Little did we know, the timing couldn't have been better: the upcoming local and statewide elections were about to create an earthquake that would leave the national education landscape forever shifted.

From the time that George Pataki took office as governor of New York in January 1995, he set his sights on shaking up education. In January 1998, Pataki, a moderate Republican, put forward a state budget proposal that included a charter school law for New York. We had been waiting and hoping for this. In the seven years that had passed since the first charter law was signed in Minnesota, in 1991, thirty-three additional states had passed charter laws of their own.

Nobody expected an easy road when it came to passing the New York State Charter Schools Act. As Governor Pataki would later explain to us, virtually no one in the state legislature was firmly on his side. The Republicans by and large did not like the idea, he told us, because they were primarily focused on securing additional funds for suburban school districts they represented. The Democrats didn't like it because they received most of their financial support from the teachers' unions. The teachers' unions didn't like it because it threatened their status quo. In conventional public schools, tenure is granted to virtually all teachers, and it's very rare that a tenured teacher is fired. There is also very little monetary incentive for teachers to work harder than is necessary, because union contracts prohibit incentive pay. Also, very few public schools have been closed for poor performance or mismanagement. Charters schools turn every one of those ideas on their heads. Should a charter school not achieve the goals set out in their charter, they could be—and often were—closed. Should teachers or administrators not perform well, they could be fired.

It was therefore not surprising that Pataki's proposal was met with fierce opposition in Albany. The Democrats who controlled the state legislature joined the teachers' union and school administrators in championing the status quo and blocked Pataki's charter law.

But Pataki wasn't about to give up, and Joe and I found it almost entertaining to watch the governor tango toward a deal with the Democrats that December. More brazen it could not have been: Legislators had spent a lot of time and effort pushing for a law to raise their salaries from $59,500 to $79,500 on January 1, 1999. If the pay raise was not passed in December, 1998, then the legislators could not receive their raise for two more years. Pataki made it clear that he was ready to veto the pay raise—unless, of course, a deal could be struck. Brazen it may have been, but we learned this is how business gets done in New York.

In the end, the salary of the legislators was increased to $79,500 and the children of New York got a charter school law allowing for the creation of one hundred charter schools. Under the law, two separate government entities were given the power to authorize new charter schools: the Board of Regents, whose members were all appointed by the State Assembly, and the State University of New York (SUNY), whose trustees were appointed by the governor. This second authorizer was an important achievement. The State Assembly was firmly under the control of the teachers' union, which opposed charters. Absent a second authorizer, it was unlikely that many charter schools would be created. The charter law also included the provision that new charter schools with fewer than 250 students would not be required to unionize. Although New York came late to the party, we were blessed with one of the best charter laws.

We still think it's amazing that Pataki was able to get the charter law through despite so many obstacles, but when we met with him years later to discuss how he did it, he presented his accomplishment as simply being a sensible course of action. It was an elegant description: "Competition works and choice works," he told us. "So in education a logical step was to have competition. . . . It was something I felt very strongly about."

———

While we've mostly voted Democrat, we've had many friends far more conservative than us, and for many years Joe had been working alongside conservatives in his position on the board of directors of the Manhattan Institute for Policy Research, a New York City—

based conservative think tank. The Manhattan Institute had created the Center for Educational Innovation (CEI) in 1990 under the leadership of Sy Fliegel and Coleman Genn, two long-time reformers and small school advocates who were leaders in the turnaround of District 4 in East Harlem led by Superintendent Tony Alvarado. Sy and Col are true heroes in the New York school reform story. Col, when Superintendent of a district in Queens, had worn a wire for several months to reveal the criminal activities of his Board at great personal risk to himself. Sadly Col passed away in 2004 but Sy, now in his 80's, is still pushing reform with great energy and success. Joe was first exposed to CEI by Manhattan Institute's Chairman, Roger Hertog, soon after CEI was formed in 1989. It was created with the impetus coming from several very conservative trustees led by Hertog, Dick Gilder, Bruce Kovner and Peter Flanigan. Joe had known most of these men from his Wall Street days except for Peter whom we met when we became fellow IHAD sponsors. Peter and I agreed on nothing political but we shared a love of opera. Joe and I developed great respect for Peter as we watched him care for his wife Bridget for over a decade during her incapacitating illness. He went on to create the Student Sponsor Partnership which has provided thousands of scholarships to Catholic high schools for inner city children most of them non-Catholic.

Seeing these right wing Republicans leading the fight for public education reform turned my views of politics upside down. It didn't make sense to us that Democrats did not support charter schools, as the beneficiaries of charters and school choice were primarily African-American and Latino families, who historically vote Democrat. But the legislature's Black and Puerto Rican Caucus—all of whom were Democrats—had been co-opted by the teachers' union and therefore opposed charters. Equally surprising to me was widespread liberal opposition led by the *New York Times*. Our positive experience with Jack Rosenthal, Joe Berger and Dith Pran reflected the concern for inner city minority children of three caring men and not the views of their newspaper which either ignored or criticized efforts to change the broken system. Readers of the *Post* and the *Daily News* learned much more about charters than those of the *Times*. The *New York Sun*, formed in 2001 by the leaders at Manhattan Institute, also supported education reform and charters.

When it came to education, the conservatives who sponsored CEI and helped to pass the Charter law were mainly focused on vouchers and education tax credits. Vouchers are certificates issued by the government that parents can apply toward tuition at a private school rather than at the public school to which their child is assigned. An alternative to the education voucher is the education tax credit, which allows individuals to use their own money to pay for the education of their children or to donate money toward the education of other children. The issue of vouchers became hotly contested—and highly political. Because students could use vouchers to attend religiously affiliated private schools, the issue raised the question of separation of church and state. The Manhattan Institute supported the idea of school vouchers. But as the public started to view vouchers as anti-union, anti–public schools, and potentially religiously biased, they became a fall-on-your-sword issue. New York, along with many other states, had passed so called Blaine Amendments in the late 19th Century which constitutionally prohibited public funds being used to support private school education. CEI, which was a part of the Institute, was a strong proponent of charters and had no interest in the voucher war. Opponents of reform tended to include charters and vouchers as a similar evil. For CEI to flourish, it could no longer be affiliated with Manhattan Institute. CEI merged with an older, somewhat inactive reform group, the Public Education Association. The combined organization, now known as CEI-PEA was spun off by Manhattan Institute in 2000.

It was these same leaders at the Manhattan Institute who first approached Joe in 1999 with the idea that we take the lead in moving the charter movement to the political center. They realized that for charters to be successful they had to have a broad base of support and not be seen as a creature of the Republican right. CEI-PEA had not yet been spun off, and I guess they saw us as moderates with no ties to the Republican Party. Our first response to this idea was: *Us? Are you kidding?* We were in our mid-sixties by this time, and had five grandchildren. Most of our friends had retired and were spending their time doing all of the things they had put on hold during their working years. It was probably time for us to do the same, or at least for us to begin to slow down.

At the same time, we had to agree that this idea made sense, and we knew that if charters were to truly succeed, broader political support was necessary. We sat with the idea for awhile, and more and more often, we found ourselves discussing different ideas of what the future of the charter school movement might look like, and what our role could be.

In October 1999, we flew to California to speak at an education conference of the NewSchools Venture Fund at the Stanford Graduate School of Business, where Joe had earned his MBA just after serving in the navy. Here a lot of the discussion revolved around a desire to expand the charter school movement by engaging "social entrepreneurs" and "venture philanthropists" (terms we were not familiar with at the time).

The powerhouse venture capitalist outfit Kleiner Perkins Caufield & Byers was sponsoring the conference. One of its partners, John Doerr, started the fund with a young Stanford Graduate School of Business student named Kim Smith, whose parents had both worked in education. Kim had worked with Wendy Kopp at Teach For America before going to California to get her MBA. When we went to see Kim on that visit in 1999, she steered us toward an interesting man named Reed Hastings, saying we needed to talk to him and listen to his ideas about charter schools and education.

Hastings had done a brief turn in the marines before joining the Peace Corps and teaching high school math in Swaziland. He made a fortune from the first company he founded, Pure Software, when it was acquired for a reported $750 million. The sale of that company gave him some time to think about what he wanted to do with himself. Like us, he chose education.

"After Pure Software, I had a bunch of money, and I didn't really want to buy yachts and such things," he told the *Wall Street Journal* in 2008. "I wanted to find something important to do. And I started looking at education, trying to figure out why our education is lagging when our technology is increasing at great rates and there's great innovation in so many other areas—health care, biotech, information technology, movie-making. Why not education?"

So Reed got himself appointed to the California Board of Education and used the money he had accumulated to become a major education philanthropist. But it was his ideas, not his money, that impressed us. He told us, when we met him in 1999, that he believed if charter schools could account for 10 percent of the students in a given district, that would constitute the necessary critical mass necessary for charters to have a dramatic impact on all public schools. This was the year before author Malcolm Gladwell published his book *The Tipping Point: How Little Things Can Make a Big Difference* and introduced the idea to a much larger audience. We both liked Hastings and thought he was an asset to the charter movement.

We were greatly inspired by what we'd learned in California, and believed that the charter school movement was at a real turning point. We began to think about all of the people in the educational reform movement who had inspired us through the years, and who we really respected: people like Wendy Kopp, the founder and CEO of Teach For America. Wendy first proposed the creation of Teach For America in her undergraduate senior thesis at Princeton University in 1989, and has spent the years since working to grow the organization's impact. Under her leadership, Teach For America's nearly thirty-three thousand participants—who commit to a two-year teaching position—have reached more than three million children nationwide. The young people they have been able to recruit are truly exemplary. For example, in a recent year, incoming teachers earned an average GPA of 3.6. One-third of incoming corps members were people of color, and 31 percent received Federal Pell Grants. Nearly 48,000 people applied in 2011, 12 percent of Ivy League seniors applied, as did 10 percent of seniors at Howard University, 8 percent at the University of Michigan-Ann Arbor, and 5 percent at the University of Texas at Austin. Teach For America's success in attracting high achievers into the teaching profession has been truly amazing, considering the resistance it has had to overcome. In a little more than twenty years, Teach For America alums have stood among the leaders in education reform, and we've long supported the tremendous work that Wendy does, both personally and financially.

Two alumni of her program, David Levin and Mike Feinberg, had also been quite an inspiration to us. In 1994, they founded the Knowledge Is Power Program (KIPP), which has grown into a national network of high performing charter schools. Their work started when Mike and David launched a fifth-grade public school program in inner-city Houston, Texas, after completing their commitment to Teach For America. In 1995, Feinberg remained in Houston to lead KIPP Academy Middle School, and Levin returned home to New York City to establish KIPP Academy New York in the South Bronx. These two original KIPP academies became the starting place for a growing network of public schools that have transformed the lives of students in under-resourced communities, and they have redefined the notion of what is possible in public education. Doris and Don Fisher, cofounders of Gap Inc., formed a partnership with Feinberg and Levin to replicate the success of the two original KIPP academies by training aspiring school leaders to open and operate new KIPP schools. In 2011–2012, more than half of KIPP school leaders are Teach For America alumni.

KIPP students have a sustained track records of high student achievement. According to a 2010 study by the research group Mathematica, KIPP middle school students make statistically significant academic gains in math and reading. More than 90 percent of KIPP alumni go on to college-preparatory high schools. While less than 40 percent of low-income students attend college nationally, 84 percent of students who complete 8th grade at KIPP matriculate to college.

Norm Atkins, whose Newark charter school we'd gone to visit a few years earlier, was also proving to be a real entrepreneur in education reform. Norm founded Uncommon Schools, a nonprofit charter management organization (CMO) recognized for starting and operating among the highest performing urban schools in the nation. He would also go on to co-create the Relay Graduate School of Education, a groundbreaking institution of higher education designed specifically to train and develop urban public school teachers. One of the great schools created by Uncommon was Excellence Charter School founded by John King, who went on to become New York State Education Commissioner in 2011. John is the first African American to hold that post. Uncommon's principal backer was Paul Tudor Jones, who like us, had been an IHAD sponsor. Paul then founded the Robin Hood Foundation which became the largest funder of charter schools in New York City. Robin Hood, whose sole mission is fighting poverty in New York City, now raises and spends $180 million annually on this mission. Paul thinks big. We first learned that in the late 1980's when we proudly took our Dreamers to Lime Rock race track in northwest Connecticut only to learn that Paul had taken his entire group to East Africa on safari.

What we find inspiring about people like Wendy, Mike, David, and Norm is the entrepreneurial spirit they have all brought to education reform. The same goes for many of the venture philanthropists who have become big funders of charter schools. Most of them are first-generation philanthropists. They are giving away money they themselves have earned and are not answerable to trustees who must use caution giving away funds entrusted to them by people who are no longer living. This makes them more willing to take risks. They are people like Paul Tudor Jones and Julian Robertson, a friend of many years who made the money he now donates through the Robertson Foundation. Julian created Tiger Management which in turn created the Tiger Foundation. He taught a generation of Tiger cubs working for him who went on to start their own firms and their own Foundations. The same is true for the people behind the Robin Hood Foundation who have followed Paul Tudor Jones' leadership.

After many long discussions about the matter, Joe and I began to see that so many people had forged the trail with us, and maybe we did have a greater responsibility. After all, wasn't this what we had always wanted: to have our ten years of effort change the education playing field? Now here it was, a real possibility to make that happen on a broader scale. Reed Hastings's ideas made sense to us, and the new law meant an altered set of circumstances. We had spent a decade fighting the system, trying to make possible changes that would enable schools to be run for the benefit of the students and their families. When we started, we'd thought this ordering of priorities was a self-evident concept. A decade of bruises taught us a great deal. Now with the charter law we had a legal basis on which to move forward. We thought about the age issue and decided it could be an advantage to be the "grandparents" of the movement. We knew and had the trust of many of the funders. Having started one of the first schools, we understood the challenges and could relate to the entrepreneurs who would start most of these charter schools. Our challenge became to organize our allies, encourage the bureaucrats to support the new law, and help develop the leadership to take movement forward.

So, in the end, despite the part of us that felt somewhat inclined to leave all of this to others and go spend more time with our family, a louder voice prevailed. It told us this was no time to quit, that all we had been fighting for now seemed possible. We listened to that voice, and so began another decade of struggle to turn an idea into a movement.

# EIGHT

# THE POWER OF BUREAUCRACY

## *Joe*

**W**e took stock of our situation. We realized we had to make some important strategic decisions about our own future and that of the Beginning with Children Foundation. If we were going to organize and build the movement, it meant we would be spending less time at Beginning with Children Foundation, so we would have to strengthen that organization. Before we could move on to the broader challenge, we had to get our own business in order, a task that would end up taking the better part of three years.

Our then-executive director, Laura Bell, a reading specialist, had worked with Carol at the Lexington School for the Deaf and joined Beginning with Children Foundation when we began. Laura was a superb educator and was a strong, positive force in setting high standards at the Beginning with Children School. In the early years, there had often been differences between the foundation and the school, and Laura was adamant in maintaining the high standards she had helped to set, even when this did not win her any popularity contests at the school. Based on her strength as an educator, we decided in 1996 to make her the executive director, hoping she would develop the necessary management skills to direct the organization. That, alas, had not happened quickly—or not in our estimation, anyway. As a result, friction developed between us. Laura chose to resign in late 1999, and we instituted a search for her successor. Through this search process, we found and hired Mimi Clarke Corcoran. She had worked for George Soros's Open Society Institute, helping to establish nongovernmental organizations in Eastern Europe and to create The After School Corporation. She became the new executive director of the Beginning with Children Foundation in April 2000.

Mimi, unfortunately, began her job with us during one of the roughest periods in our history. Not long after the murder of Tony, our four-year-old student, Carol and I had decided we wanted to do more for the community and expand our efforts in South Williamsburg in two major ways: grow the school to incorporate a middle school, up to the eighth grade; and build a community center that could act as a meeting place for people in the neighborhood, even for families whose children did not attend Beginning with Children. Tony's death had had a profound effect on us, and—not unlike when, ten years earlier, we'd heard our Dreamers referred to as garbage, we knew that in many ways our work had just begun.

We had gone to our partner Pfizer and told them of our plans. The company had always been a wonderful, consistent supporter, and this time was no different. Not only did they fully back our plan, they even offered us the entire city block on which the school was located, and a grant of $750,000 toward the creation of the middle school and the community center. The plan included the renovation of the original Pfizer headquarters' office built into community meeting rooms and a small Pfizer museum commemorating the 150th anniversary of its founding. Perhaps even more important, top management at Pfizer also offered us the political support we knew would be critical for such a complex project that required the approval and cooperation of several public agencies at both the city and state levels.

The first political assistance Pfizer offered us seemed like a huge break. Brooklyn was represented on the Board of Education by a man named William C. Thompson, who had been appointed by our friend and supporter, Brooklyn Borough President Howard Golden. Thompson's appointment had been pushed by Pfizer—obviously a plus for us—and Thompson had just been elected President of the Board, which greatly enhanced his ability to get things done in Brooklyn. With Tom Kline, we went to meet Thompson, and to tell him of our plans.

His response was better than we could have imagined.

Thompson fully supported our plans, and had an idea of his own. "School construction is a big mess," Thompson said. "Why don't we have you build it privately? After all, you have shown us you know how to educate better than the board." We couldn't disagree with this sentiment, and we knew the city very much liked what we were doing in South Williamsburg. In fact, in 1997, Beginning with Children was named the most improved elementary school in New York City and presented with a Literacy Hero Award by Mayor Rudolph Giuliani. That same year, we had also been asked to participate as a pilot school in the chancellor's School-Based Budgeting Initiative. Rudy Crew, who assumed the chancellorship after Ray Cortines, was interested in establishing school-based budgeting, and we believed our private sector experience gave us a valuable perspective. It had been frustrating for us to receive funds designated for a specific purpose that bore no relation to the specific needs of our school. Although talented principals often could manipulate the system to move funds around, we were interested in changing the system so the funds that came into our school could be allocated to the areas where they were truly needed. We prepared a budget that made no changes in the amount of dollars to be allocated to us: the only change was in the specifics of how this funding would be broken down, namely, based on the specific needs of our school. We proposed that we would create a system, and if the Board of Education saw that it was working for us, it could try the same system with other schools. We agreed to hire and pay a national accounting firm to audit our books. We committed to post a bond to cover any shortfall that might arise, so the Board of Education would be protected if we had any overruns. We organized our thinking into a proposal we thought was a big win-win and confidently took off for 110 Livingston Street, the Board of Education headquarters.

To add a note of levity, we purchased T-shirts emblazoned with the words SCHOOL BASED BUDGETING, which everyone on our team wore. We were the first to arrive in the designated conference room, and we took the opportunity to distribute T-shirts to the arriving officials. Soon the room was filled with twenty somber men and women, none of whom seemed inclined to don the T-shirt. These twenty bureaucrats were the leaders of every department of the Board of Education and their assistants. Harry Spence, deputy chancellor for operations, who had recently come to New York from Massachusetts and was an advocate of the idea, invited us to make our presentation. When we finished, he asked for comments from the people in the room. They were uniformly negative. Spence thanked us and we left. That was the end of the school-based budgeting idea. No bureaucrat wanted to relinquish any authority. They cared not a whit about the merits of the idea—something neither we nor Harry Spence considered. A few months later, Harry resigned to return to Massachusetts. He graciously invited us to his going-away party, attended by many of those same bureaucrats heaving a collective sigh of relief.

When Thompson first suggested that we build the community center ourselves, we balked. The battle to pass a state charter school bill was under way at that time, and no version of it provided any capital for charter school construction. After long discussions and much consideration, we had decided that if the state law passed and we could overcome the construction capital issue, we would attempt to convert Beginning with Children to a charter school. The biggest reason behind our decision was the fact that the charter bill codified many of the unique freedoms we had created and validated—the lottery, independence, and accountability. The bill created an opportunity for New York to have many schools like Beginning with Children. Schools would be funded on a per-child basis, permitting the school's leadership to allocate funds. We believed that, since we'd been among the leaders of the battle to gain these freedoms, it was important for us to participate.

Chancellor Crew opposed the charter bill, but he told us that if it passed he wanted good charter schools, and he urged us to convert Beginning with Children. Both he and Thompson assured us that we could close on the contracts for expansion before we applied for a charter, ensuring the expansion plans would be protected.

The benefits of converting plus these assurances outweighed the major negative: as a conversion, we would have to remain unionized, meaning we'd be responsible for the retirement and health care benefits provided in the union contract, paying them out of our per-pupil allocation. The new, non-union charters would get the same revenue but would not carry this financial burden. We underestimated how rapidly these costs would accelerate in the ensuing decade—an expensive mistake. But we forged ahead, and decided to build the new project ourselves. Armed with the support of Crew and Thompson, we went to the New York City Partnership, New York's business organization investment fund, where I had become director of the education effort and a Director of its newly formed New York City Investment Fund which had as its mission job creation in New York, primarily in the outer boroughs. The investors in the fund included most of the City's leading business organizations.

The Partnership's President and CEO Kathryn S. Wylde was an old friend who had managed the Partnership's housing efforts on Pfizer land. With her help we enlisted Fisher Brothers to do the construction, and Fisher in turn hired the architects whose managing partner was a person we had known for years. The Partnership also enlisted investment bankers to market the securities that would pay for the project, which was estimated to cost nearly $10 million. When we were finished, we would be able to accommodate 150 more students, and have a community facility that could provide an array of services for the area's families, a group much larger than just the Beginning with Children parents. We also hoped that educating and enfranchising this many families could prevent the corruption that had plagued South Williamsburg, and put an end to Wild Bill Rogers and his equally dishonest successors.

Things seemed to be going perfectly, and we envisioned another major success that could lead the way for other organizations to follow.

Another lesson learned: never underestimate the power of the bureaucracy to maintain the status quo. The Division of School Facilities, which had been our nemesis in the first construction project had new leadership but was hostage to the same blob mentality of the prior regime. Our way of doing things was a threat to the old ways, and seeing their empire threatened, the department began to insert itself into the project and set up roadblocks at every turn.

Our first bad break came when Mayor Giuliani decided to fire Chancellor Crew. Giuliani's education policy had been one of generally obstructing the bureaucrats at the board. His two allotted votes and the near automatic support of the Staten Island nominee were not enough for him to run the seven person Board, but they did aid in stopping things he didn't like, and one of the things he didn't like was the chancellor who held the job when Giuliani was elected, Ray

Cortines. Cortines, who had helped us go from a division of Eastern District High School to a full-fledged school, was a fine educator. He was not, however, cut out for New York City politics. (But, really, what humanist *is?*)

Rudy Crew, Cortines's Guiliani-picked replacement, was smart and tough but he, too, eventually got in Giuliani's way, tangling with him on the issue of school vouchers. He was terminated after five years on the job, in late 1999. The board had trouble appointing a successor. Giuliani was, at that time, campaigning for school vouchers, the bugaboo of the Democrats and the teachers' union, and had everyone very upset and agitated. He was pushing for Joseph P. Viteritti, a moderately conservative professor whom Giuliani believed would support his voucher program if appointed chancellor.

Thompson was in opposition to the mayor. He was able to get four votes for his choice, Harold Levy, the former director of global compliance at Citigroup who had been a member of the New York State Board of Regents, and Levy was named the Chancellor. At first we felt positively about Levy's appointment. He had a Wall Street background, and had, like both of us, gone to Cornell. We assumed, therefore, that we'd be able to work with him. This turned out to be a spectacularly misguided assumption.

On the Friday of Memorial Day weekend in 2000, we had just hired Mimi Corcoran as our new executive director and thought we were on our way to getting our business in good order. And then everything we'd been working so hard for was blown apart when Carol got a call from a reporter at the *New York Daily News*. The reporter said she had heard we were building on polluted ground. At this time, the land had been cleared by the New York State Department of Environmental Conservation. Architectural plans had been completed and then redone to conform to the projected cost. Fisher Brothers was ready to get underway, and the financing appeared solid. What the reporter was saying was outrageously false. We were well into the project. We would have known if this was the case. It was simply untrue. At first we were just stunned. Then we became infuriated.

"Where did you get that information?" Carol asked the reporter.

"The chancellor," she replied.

The *chancellor?*

Carol called Harold Levy and was firm in stating our displeasure. Levy agreed to visit the school that evening and meet with Pfizer's engineers, on Tuesday after the holiday weekend.

After hearing Pfizer's presentation, which was quite convincing, Levy announced he would give his decision the next day. The following morning he phoned and told us he had decided to cancel the project.

It was infuriating and heartbreaking, and Carol and I felt totally dejected. We pointed out our foundation's investment in this project, which by then had climbed to more than $2 million. These funds had been raised from our base of contributors, which included several foundations that supported education reform, and from Pfizer's original contribution of $750,000 along with the land and the existing 1849 building.

He told us that this was our misfortune, since we had no formal written contract. We then turned to Bill Thompson, who had encouraged us to undertake this project in the first place. He explained that he had fought hard to get Levy the job and could not overturn his first major decision. Thompson was planning to run for city Comptroller in 2001, and he assured us that he would make the foundation whole on its investment before leaving the Board of Education to begin his campaign. We were never so much as able to get him on the phone again after that.

We still blame ourselves for not fighting back right away against this travesty. Our mistake was in refraining to march on 110 Livingston Street, the Board of Education headquarters, with an angry, vocal, sign-waving crowd of several hundred parents from Brooklyn making a stink about getting screwed over by the bureaucrats in Manhattan. That would have made the *New York Post*. It would have made the *New York Daily News*. It might well have made NY 1 News and the *New York Times*, too. But we did not go that route. We wanted to negotiate in good faith. We went ahead with a scheduled parents' meeting for that night and did not go to war. We wish we could have that decision back now. Sometimes you have to do what is necessary if you are going to carry the day. Sometimes you have to play rough.

Most of our partners understood our plight and made reasonable settlements. The only exception was the architects. Having designed a plan that did not meet our budget, they then designed another one and charged us for both. We explained our plight. They filed suit. We were forced to pay them.

One good thing did emerge out of this terrible experience. Mayor Giuliani urged us to continue our battle for a financial settlement, and we brought suit against the City of New York for breach of promise. In settlement, the city reimbursed about 50 percent of the total project expenditures, allocated a floor in a partially empty school building near Beginning with Children, and fixed it up for us to use for our middle school. This prevented us from achieving our dream of building an integrated community center. But this arrangement did establish the concept of shared space for charter schools, a precedent that has been followed many times since and has been key to the growth of charters in New York City.

The meat market in West Virginia circa 1950 where Joe worked when he was 15 years old.

ABOVE:
Joe and Carol at Cornell University circa 1954.

RIGHT:
Joe in his Navy uniform circa 1955.

Joe and Carol Reich in front of Beginning with Children, Pfizer's old headquarters in Williamsburg. CREDIT: Dith Pran, *The New York Times Redux.*

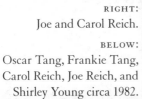

RIGHT:
Joe and Carol Reich.

BELOW:
Oscar Tang, Frankie Tang, Carol Reich, Joe Reich, and Shirley Young circa 1982.

In the library of Beginning
with Children circa 1998.

Dr. Ingrid S. Aponte.

Joe and Carol at his 70th Birthday Party.

# NINE

# A NEW HOPE

## CAROL

The other issue that took up a lot of our time was our decision to start a second school—a charter school, in the Fort Greene section of Brooklyn. After we won the Literacy Hero Award in 1997, we were approached by several groups from around the city, who asked us to help create similar schools in their community. At the time, we had neither the resources nor the political will to help everyone achieve what we did with Beginning with Children, but we had been particularly impressed by a group of a half-dozen African-American parents in Fort Greene. Led by a federal judge and several other professionals whose own educations gave them insights into just what would be needed to start a new school, the group was very committed to opening a similar school in its community. But since their district superintendent was about as welcoming as Rogers, we knew success was very unlikely.

However, after the New York State Charter Law passed in 1998 and there was a legally sanctioned path to create a new school like Beginning with Children, we decided to work with these parents to begin the Community Partnership Charter School in Fort Greene. We guided them in a variety of ways: We helped them write their charter application, a document as large and weighty as the New York City telephone directory, and assisted in the many revisions required by the authorizers. We selected the authorizer, choosing the tougher but more charter-friendly SUNY. We recruited directors for the new corporation (every charter has to be a separately incorporated 501(c)3 organization). We also helped select the school's leader and staff, and helped organize the first year's lottery. Unlike when we started Beginning with Children, this lottery was heavily oversubscribed. Several of the founding parents' children did not win places in the school, a sad consequence of the structure of the law.

The Community Partnership Charter School was approved by the SUNY's Board of Trustees in January 2000, and by the Board of Regents in April of that year. It opened in the fall of 2000, in a carriage house on Clermont Avenue, with one hundred students enrolled in two classes of kindergarten and first grade. Its charter outlined the following goals: During its allotted five years, the school would to grow to serve 250 students in grades kindergarten through sixth. Its mission was to create a strong academic base; involve families, educators, and community members; educate students to perform at levels that exceeded the citywide averages; and foster an environment that values kindness and respect.

As all of this was happening, we were also in the process of applying to convert our school to the Beginning with Children Charter School. The law required that our conversion be approved by a majority of the school's parents, which we had no trouble securing. The conversion was approved and completed in September 2001, making our school the first K-8 conversion public charter school in New York State.

After we became a charter school, not much changed in our day-to-day operations. Funding now came on the prescribed per-student basis—unlike before, when the school received funds from the Board of Education on some unknown basis. Many of the things we had been doing now had to be done according to the law. This meant that the lottery I devised a decade earlier, which strove for a balance of gender and ethnicity, was now a lottery in which the first fifty names drawn were granted admission, regardless of what the eventual makeup of the class would be. This created some weird anomalies, where one year the entering class was 80 percent boys! The law did allow us to continue the existing policy of granting preference to the siblings of existing students. That preference was very significant at Beginning with Children, which was now ten years old, and often the entering class was almost all siblings. As with the Community Partnership Charter School, we had to have a formal board of trustees for the school instead of our previous advisory board. In an effort to insure we had a broad representation of stakeholders, we divided the members into four groups: teachers, parents, our foundation, and the community. This attempt to insure democracy was a mistake. Each class of directors tended to act for the group that had nominated them and not for the needs of the school. It also created an anomalous situation where the teachers, as board members, were evaluating the principal. As time wore on, the defects in this structure resulted in paralysis on the board of Beginning with Children Charter School.

———

By this time, three years had passed since New York City had adopted the charter law and, to put it bluntly, the charter school movement was a mess, filled with widespread confusion and chaos. About a dozen charter schools had come into being during that time, but there were important differences between these schools and the support they received. One school, attracted some 80 percent of the philanthropic capital. This school received such an outsize flow of dollars because its founder, had previously worked with people from the Manhattan Institute and had a great base of support. That was how charter funding worked at this point: It was willy-nilly, not organized or thought-out. Who you knew was everything. Promising schools that had just opened were already in trouble because of a shortage of funds. The shortage occurred because the law did not include facilities funding and discounted per-pupil funding coming from the State.

The New York City charter movement had other serious problems beyond funding. Mainly, Harold Levy, the schools chancellor, was not a supporter of charter schools. Few schools were being started, and those that were could not rely on any mechanism to assist them in planning and start-up. Under Levy, the charter office at the Board of Education was an ignored stepchild with large staff turnover and no senior management support. The State Education Department, a sorry, bloated agency under control of the Regents, was also anti-charter. It approved few charters and had no quality measures. Governor Pataki had wisely created a second authorizer, the SUNY Charter School Institute. Although it became one of the country's exemplary authorizers under the leadership of executive director James D. Merriman, it was still in start-up mode.

These issues had made it clear to many people in the New York charter movement that if charter schools were truly going to succeed, a coordinated effort was needed: an organization to support all charter schools in the city with capital, advocacy, and initiatives. Yes, there were problems, but there was also a sense of real possibility. It was very clear to us, and to other educational reformers, that if some of the obvious problems and inevitable growing pains of the charter movement could be resolved, we just might be able to expand the conversation about education reform on a much broader scale. In addition to the fact that certain schools received a majority of the philanthropic support, and that the process of applying to open a charter school was cumbersome and difficult, one of the major problems stemmed from the fact that charters were not receiving support from the Schools Chancellor, Harold Levy. That needed to change before any real reform could happen.

Little did we know that change—*real* change—was just around the corner.

Despite the growing number of charter schools being established throughout New York City, charter schools were not a major issue in the 2001 campaign for New York City mayor. The *New York Times* did a major piece on the education policies of the various candidates, including Fernando Ferrer, Mark Green, Herman Badillo, and Michael Bloomberg, concluding, "Even charter schools, embraced by Republicans and Democrats elsewhere, have barely been discussed by mayoral candidates of either party."

The date of that article? September 10, 2001. One day later everyone in the city—and everywhere else—would have other things on their minds than schools.

Bloomberg narrowly won the election that November and pledged to bring the city back to life after the September 11 attacks. Of all the remarkable aspects of that horrible day in New York history, full of heroism and bravery under the most challenging of circumstances, we like to remind people that of the city's 1.2 million schoolchildren, every single one returned home safely.

Mayor Bloomberg had one clear primary objective when it came to education policy: to reverse the decline in student achievement in impoverished neighborhoods. Immediately upon taking office, he showed that he was willing to take bold transformational steps, threaten the status quo, and challenge the educational establishment.

After so many years of running into brick walls and numbing bureaucratic delays at every turn, we thought this was almost too good to be true.

Bloomberg's approach to reforming education was deceptively simple: He focused first on taking back control. He wanted the state legislature in Albany to grant him control of New York City's schools, starting with the right to make his own appointment for schools chancellor, and in June 2002, he succeeded in getting that landmark change passed.

Mayor Bloomberg wasted no time in proving just how willing he was to think entirely out of the box. In late July, Bloomberg announced that his new schools chancellor was a man with neither the background nor the baggage of a career educator: Joel Klein. At the time, Klein was the chairman and CEO of Bertelsmann, Inc., the U.S. arm of the German publishing giant, but he was best known for taking on Microsoft when he was assistant attorney general, overseeing the Department of Justice's Antitrust Division from 1997 to 2001.

Many people in New York's education circles scratched their heads at the choice of Joel. After all, his education experience was limited to a brief stint teaching sixth grade at a Long Island City public school, after he himself was educated in New York's public school system.

Joel was used to being underestimated, and to proving people wrong. As *Time* magazine noted in a 1997 article with the headline "The Trustbuster Who Roared," "When Joel Klein came up for approval as chief of the Justice Department's antitrust division last summer, even some Democratic Senators viewed him as a doormat for Big Business and tried to step on his appointment. All that changed last week when Klein audaciously hauled mighty Microsoft into court."

His selection as New York City Schools Chancellor was such a closely guarded secret that not even top aides to Bloomberg knew about it until shortly before the press conference that announced his appointment. It turned out that both Klein and the mayor were friends of the writer Margaret Carlson, who covered four presidential campaigns for *Time* magazine and was also the first woman columnist in that magazine's history. She introduced the two and made sure their paths would cross at more than one social occasion.

"Mutual friends and others told Mayor Bloomberg about this passion I have about education," Joel told us later. "He called me and asked me if I would I like to talk to him and some people on his team. There were four or five people in the room, and they asked me all kinds of questions. What was my vision? What were my concerns? What are the important changes?"

"I kept reading in the papers about different people who had been interviewed, and I assumed I wouldn't get the job. Two months later, I was hired. Mike always jokes that the reason I got the job was that I was the only guy who didn't leak to the newspapers that he had been interviewed. I always joked back that the reason I got the job was because it was so implausible to think I would get it that nobody would believe me even if I leaked it."

The announcement of Joel as chancellor may have caught many by surprise, but no one questioned that Joel was smart, thought for himself, and was ready to take on the powerful: entrenched interests of the education blob and their political supporters. And, even more, no one questioned that he was clearly taking this job out of a heartfelt and passionate desire to make a difference—especially not after he talked about his New York public school education on the day he was announced.

"I owe those teachers, and this city school system, more than I can ever repay," he said. "I pledge to do all that I can to give each child in the City of New York a first-rate education and the keys to unlock what this magnificent world has to offer. . . . Let me add a word to the parents of all our school children. I know how much you care about your children's education. I know personally what it is like to look into the eyes of an infant and be filled with hopes and dreams. We cannot let those hopes and dreams be dashed by an educational system that does not give our kids what they need and deserve."

Joel was a polarizing figure, no question about that. At the outset we, like many others, were not sure what to make of him. What we did know was that when Joel Klein committed himself to something, he was in it all the way and would follow up to a T. What we did not know was where he stood on charter schools, or how he saw the future of New York City public education. Soon enough we would see just how visionary and passionate he was about rethinking and reshaping our approach to educating the young.

"I believe deeply in the transformative power of education," Joel told us later. "I grew up in an environment where there wasn't a lot of joy. Mine was not an easy family. There wasn't a lot of income. Through education I found a pathway to an entirely different, quite unimagined life. I consider myself the luckiest person alive. Teachers changed my life. I have been through some very tough times in my life, personal times."

"I wouldn't say I had a well-thought-through vision when I started as chancellor. But I had some core concepts. It was more of a case of knowing what I thought did not work. People were talking the same old, same old: better curriculum, more after school, more preschool, lower class size. The simple fact was that by then it had been almost twenty years since the Reagan National Commission on Excellence in Education report 'A Nation at Risk' advocated those same priorities, from 1983 to 2002, and it did not work! We put a lot of money into that effort but it hadn't worked."

The "Nation at Risk" report, published in 1983, caused a political earthquake at the time. Its commission, chaired by the formidable David Pierpont Gardner, shook up the complacency that until that time had characterized most discussions of education in this country. They presented a grim portrait of failing schools and questioned the long-held belief that any problem in education could be solved simply by allocating more funding.

"If an unfriendly power had attempted to impose on America the mediocre educational performance that exists today, we might well have viewed it as an act of war," the report stated, in language that was widely quoted.

The furor the report caused did not last long, and years later few of its recommendations had actually been implemented. As we knew far too well, old thinking and entrenched interests are as difficult to uproot as crabgrass. The folly of continuing to throw money at the problem without changing the overall approach continued.

# TEN

# ESTABLISHING THE CHARTER CENTER

## JOE

Although we had not yet met privately with Joel Klein, the speech he gave at a public gathering seemed to indicate that he might be pro-charter. All of us in the charter movement waited with a lot of anticipation to see where Joel would eventually land on charter schools, and we knew that real opportunities for progress awaited us if we could bring charters to his attention. Two funders, Phoebe Boyer of the Tiger Foundation and Chuck Hamilton of the Clark Foundation, organized a meeting, at Pocantico Hills, New York, in December 2002, of twenty-five current and potential charter funders, in hopes of having a frank discussion about the way forward. Carol and I were asked to give the keynote address. We were the only people who were both funders and operators of charter schools, and we had a unique perspective. In the weeks leading up to the meeting, we prepared our remarks and readied ourselves to make a pitch for the idea constructed by us and Mimi Corcoran: a charter center.

When we arrived at Pocantico Hills, a beautiful area of rolling hills and lush farms about an hour north of New York City, it felt like we had arrived at a wake. The movement was severely lacking in energy, and we knew that the people who had gathered were having a difficult time seeing how we could breathe new life into it. As I took the stage to give the talk I'd entitled "The Glass Is More Than Half Full," I prepared to do whatever I could to infuse it with a fresh sense of purpose.

"Had I been speaking with you six months ago, it would have been hard to have an encouraging tone," I began. "We were then in the midst of what Bruno Manno of the Annie E. Casey Foundation called the three-front war against charters: state policy makers, local school systems, and interest groups, especially the teachers' unions and education schools."

I then detailed some of the signs we believed bolstered the case for optimism, including the indication that Chancellor Klein's views on charter schools were positive—a big contrast to the prior policy, which the bureaucracy worked very hard to undermine charter schools. We needed, therefore, to look forward with a vision unencumbered by the old burdens of disappointment and limitation. Instead of looking at charter schools as underfunded public schools where donors were asked to make up the shortfall, we should realize they have many of the same characteristics of private schools—except that they were public schools, and every dollar donated to help them would in effect be matched five-fold by public money. That was an argument for the glass being way more than half full!

I then pitched the idea for our charter center. It would, I explained, be a unique enterprise—an organization of support, not control. It would coordinate efforts among all charter funders, allowing us to speak with one voice. It would be a place where social entrepreneurs—those wanting to open a charter school in their community—could come for technical assistance in writing their charter. As everyone in that room understood, dealing with the Department of Education was like dealing with the Defense Department. Writing a charter was very complicated. When finished, it could be as thick as the New York City phone book, with two addenda of equal size. A charter center would help guide people through that process. It would also be a funding institution, providing financial support to schools for planning and start up. It would help fight the battles for space. This was a serious problem for people looking to start a charter school, as the law did not provide any money for building. It would also negotiate with the United Federation of Teachers and other unions for work rule relief.

I also emphasized the need to be as open-eyed in assessing and evaluating new charter proposals as any businessperson would be in taking a hard look at a business plan. This businesslike focus was second nature to me and would, I knew, appeal to prospective funders.

"The other enemy of the charter school movement," I said to the Pocantico audience, "has been the enemy within—poorly operated charter schools." "We have all seen them—schools without a sound financial plan making poor real estate decisions that are doomed to fail. We as funders face the horrible choice of throwing good money after bad or closing a school and uprooting deserving children. We must be more disciplined in who we fund and hold grantees to very high standards in start-up and operations."

I firmly believed that a charter center was an idea whose time had come, and that the people in that room were the ones to make it happen. With the city under new leadership and suffering from a budget crisis, the chancellor was going to reach out to the funding community. We should support him but demand something in return. The time to do that was now. "We would be happy to work with you to create this entity," I said, before turning the microphone over to Carol.

"It has been more than a half century since Brown v. Board of Education and our public schools, for the most part, continue to be abysmal," Carol began. "And those conditions unequally affect the poorest citizens of this country." She went on to explain that statistics on suicide rates among young males showed that the highest rates are among young men of color between the ages of eighteen and thirty. It is rumored that we build our prisons based on fifth-grade reading scores. These were all terrible condemnations of current education. If we had the will to bring real change to our schools, she told our colleagues, we could do it.

"Those of you who are seated around this room share that will," she said. "I know you do. So do Joe and I. If we get to work in New York, we can show the rest of the country what can be done. How does the song go about New York? If I can make it there, I can make it anywhere. If we can do it here, they can do it anywhere. Because the children don't have time to waste."

We were happy with the reception we received. We felt a sense of unity at that gathering, and left with a feeling of great support for our idea, as well as a clear awareness that we had a lot of work still left to do. That was a strange period. Change was coming, everyone knew it, but Joel Klein had yet to take a public stand on charters. It was clear that Mayor Bloomberg was the kind of leader who would set the stage for meaningful change, but who would also provide Joel with room to establish his own priorities. What we did not know yet was that our partnership with Joel Klein would take our efforts to another level in terms of impact on developments all over New York.

———

Joel turned out to be fully onboard with the idea of a charter center so much so that he was already planning the idea himself. He believed it needed to be privately funded and independent of the Department of Education. He was not sure how to proceed. He approached Russ Carson, a very successful private equity investor and philanthropist, to ask how he would recommend creating such a center.

"Do you know Joe Reich?" Russ asked Joel.

"No," Joel told him.

"You need to talk to Joe," Russ said. "He's the guy that can help you launch this thing."

Of course we were eager to meet Joel, responded immediately when he called to setup a meeting with us to talk. This was quite a rough time for Carol and me because I had recently been diagnosed with cancer. It started with a spot Carol noticed on my back, which turned out to be melanoma. My doctor then discovered that I also had lung and kidney cancer. During the course of a summer, I underwent very intensive chemotherapy treatment, and I was in the midst of these treatments when Joel arrived at our apartment for our initial meeting. It was the first time I had put on a jacket and tie in months, and we gathered in our living room. I was not at my best, it is safe to say, but the three of us had an important conversation. We both hit it off with Joel right away. He made a strong impression as a smart guy and a straight talker with a clear vision. Within a couple of months, we were talking to Joel in detail about having the city provide more space for new charter schools to open. We also told Joel that we would make a significant initial contribution to establish the charter center. This decision meant that we would step away from daily involvement in our two schools. It was our hope that the schools would continue to break new ground and be laboratories for innovation. Deciding to head in this new direction also meant that we were going to step up our personal philanthropy to help build the movement. The commitment we made to Joel represented a significant part of our total philanthropic funds. In addition, we became more significant funders of other charter schools and of educational support organizations, including Teach For America, DonorsChoose, Civic Builders, and Chess-in-the-Schools.

We astounded even ourselves when, in the space of just one week, a small group of people, including Joel, were able to raise $40 million to fund the establishment of the new Charter Center. It was a true public-private partnership between the city, the Department of Education, and private philanthropists, with the initial funding coming primarily from the Robertson Foundation, the Robin Hood Foundation, and, at a somewhat more modest level, Carol and me.

Our next step was to decide who was going to provide the initial leadership. It obviously could not be Joel Klein himself. Neither Julian Robertson, founder of the Robertson Foundation, nor Paul Tudor Jones would have made sense either, due to their significant other commitments. That narrowed it down to two choices: Carol or me.

Carol declined the opportunity to lead the Center, although she did attend every meeting. By this time, my chemotherapy treatment had been completed. I was feeling much better and eager for a new challenge. With Carol's support, I invited Joel to breakfast at the Regency Hotel in the city and laid it out for him in black and white: Joel could not be the chairman of the Charter Center. Julian was not going to be the chairman. There was only one way this was going to work. And I was more than up for the task.

Mayor Bloomberg and Chancellor Klein held a news conference in October 2003 at the Renaissance Charter School, in Queens, to announce an ambitious plan to create fifty new charter schools in New York, in all five boroughs, and to establish the charter center— which at that point was being called the New York City Center for Charter Excellence—as a nonprofit "in partnership with the private sector and not-for-profit community." The point was clear: Bloomberg and Klein were making an unprecedented push on charters. We both spoke that day, as did Caroline Kennedy.

"The creation of academically rigorous charter schools is an integral part of our overall effort to support excellence in our classrooms," Bloomberg said. "Charter schools foster innovation and attract vital new resources to our school system. The entrepreneurial and competitive nature of these schools inspires and stimulates positive change throughout our entire school system."

The announcement and press conference that day amounted to a kind of coming-out party for Joel Klein's intense commitment to charter schools, and a sort of going-public event for us. "Today's announcement is a testament to our belief that there is more than one way to deliver high-quality public education," Joel said. "Charter schools represent a tremendous opportunity to attract new resources to our public schools and to spur system-wide change. Charter schools also reflect the vision underlying the Children First reforms"—a professional development program designed by New York City to support educators by using data to inform instructional and organizational decision-making—"that strong leadership, autonomy at the school level, and accountability for performance are key to giving our children the quality education they need and deserve."

"My wife, Josie, and I love New York and think it is essential that our city's children have every educational opportunity," Julian said. "We count ourselves fortunate to have a mayor and a chancellor with the vision to believe that charter schools, working together with public schools, can make New York a model for public education in America. We are proud to join with Robin Hood and Joe and Carol Reich in support of this important initiative."

Getting the Center up and running was a significant challenge. In the first few months, we had no staff, so it was just Carol and me, working with Mimi, Phoebe, and Emary Aronson from the Robin Hood Foundation. We all knew each other well, and could work together. To get started, we needed to have an excellent CEO in place, but we soon discovered that finding strong and willing CEO candidates was no easy task. Charters remained a big unknown to most people, and although we had great plans for New York, the local charter movement heretofore had not gained tremendous momentum. Therefore, most of the candidates we recruited were skeptical. No one had ever started or run a center like this before, so the new CEO had to be entrepreneurial. We decided to accept Robin Hood's suggestion to use an executive search firm they knew well. The search soon turned into a nightmare. We kept weeding through candidates, none of whom seemed even close to right. Eventually we agreed on a man named Stefan Pryor, who had served as a vice president at the Partnership for New York City, where he focused on public education and school reform. After September 11, he went to work on the economic rehabilitation of New York at the Lower Manhattan Development Corporation. He accepted our offer, but three weeks before he was to start, Pryor called to inform us he was not taking the job.

It was six months after the Charter Center had come into being, and we still had no leader. We also had an executive search firm informing us they had no other viable candidates, and no desire to continue the search. We had no other choice but to take on the task ourselves, and soon after we began to ask around, we heard from a few contacts about one woman who might be right for this difficult job.

Paula L. Gavin had served as the president and CEO of the YMCA of Greater New York from 1990 to 2004, and in that capacity she had been responsible for a very large, sprawling organization that included twenty branches and two hundred affiliated program locations in New York. She left the Y to work for a venture capital firm and, capable as she was, in the new job she was clearly a fish out of water. She needed a change, and we needed her. In her early sixties, Paula seemed to know everybody in New York City, and she had an enormous and infectious amount of energy. She knew nothing about education and nothing about charter schools, but her intelligence and enthusiasm outweighed that. We needed to get moving, and convinced the board to hire her. Next we went out and found somebody who did know something about charter schools and could complement her, hiring as chief operating officer a man named Matt Candler. He had years of experience in charters, including starting new charters for the Knowledge Is Power Program. Paula was a whirling dervish of energy, and within three months we had an office, a business plan, and a staffed organization.

Paula's energy and contacts made her a great asset, but without a deep understanding of charter schools and, even more important, the political topography of public education, she was often surprised by what she found. During her time with the YMCA, Paula was regularly received in Albany affably, and with respect. She'd find that this was not so as the CEO of the Charter Center. Because where education and politics mixed, just about everything felt like combat. Plenty of people were against charters, then as now, and many of them could be shrill and hostile. The politics of the issue were confusing, daunting and ever changing. There were still a lot of Democratic legislators who made it a point of pride—or at least stubbornness—to oppose charters without even understanding what they were. Many insisted they were the tip of a vast right-wing conspiracy. The hope was really to strangle the charter movement in the cradle. That desire could create both a tone and dynamic that were very contentious.

# ELEVEN

# GROWING PAINS

## CAROL

Since nobody had ever attempted to create a charter center, there were no guidelines for us to follow, and we once again returned to the advice of good old Junior at the Sanitary Meat Market: do something, even if you do it wrong. And we did do a few things wrong at first, although I like to sometimes think of it as having made decisions that we later outgrew. Our theory was that we should try a lot of different things and see what worked, rather than waste time or tread water by devoting too much time to open-ended analysis of what eventually needed to be done. The $40 million we had raised was supplemented by an additional $1 million from the Clark Foundation. With that money, we had the resources to embark on a pointed effort to get programs up and running to attract good people to the charter world, and to ease their transition.

Our initial goal was to make fifty new charter schools operational in New York City—the number authorized by the 1998 law. To achieve this, we offered a variety of support programs and funding opportunities, like planning and start-up grants to groups wanting to open schools. We also worked with Joel Klein to make available shared space in public school facilities. This, of course, was an approach that we had pioneered with the Beginning with Children School, which became the first in the city to use shared space. Under Joel Klein's leadership, this concept was implemented throughout New York, and the idea of "co-location" became a major part of the discussion among charter school advocates. This one innovation was probably the single most important factor in making New York a national leader on charters.

Other efforts included funding groups like Civic Builders, which helped people build schools. We funded development organizations such as New Leaders, Building Excellent Schools, and Emerging Leaders Fellows Program, which produced school leaders. We implemented a principal-support network. We remained committed to the idea that if charter schools could educate 10 percent of the students in a given district, they could have an impact on all public schools. However, we knew that while we would not be able to reach that 10 percent on a citywide basis for a very long time, we could reach it in certain neighborhoods. So we decided to launch an effort to cluster the new schools in the three areas of greatest need: Harlem, the South Bronx, and Central Brooklyn.

We had such a great partner in Chancellor Klein. He sought out the best operators in the country and enticed them to New York with the promise of a charter-friendly administration, offering free space in existing underutilized school buildings, and all of the resources of the Charter Center. The Center's Board met at least four times a year, often more. During his tenure, Joel never missed a meeting. His active participation reflected the importance which he attached to the Center's work. This combination was made more effective by the help of entrepreneurial philanthropists, mostly from the financial community. They were attracted to charters because they could see how their funds were being used to create new, accountable entities.

The other major task we took on at the Charter Center was that of advocacy. Paula did a wonderful job speaking out and being a voice in the media. We needed to influence the battle of ideas in ways large and small. One of our major efforts, which was a bit of a headache but also a major triumph, was to bring in a highly regarded Harvard professor named Caroline Hoxby to analyze the standardized test scores of all children who had entered the charter school lottery. She compared those who had won and were attending charter schools with those who had not won a spot in the schools.

Bringing in a Harvard professor to do research might not have seemed like a controversial choice. Hoxby was an academic star renowned for her teaching. What she was not was politically correct. Many were against her and we ended up wrangling with her critics including some of our supporters over the decision to hire Caroline and how to supervise her. In the midst of this controversy, we were invited to lunch at the *New York Times*. Caroline's name came up, and one of the Times' editors referred to her as a "right wing nut case." Then we knew she was the person to do the job. For Joe, the fight over Hoxby would be one of the toughest battles he faced in his time as chairman of the Charter Center.

But in the end it was worth it, because the Hoxby's study turned out to be an extremely critical piece of research when it came to understanding the difference charter schools were making. Released in September 2009, the study found that students who entered lotteries and won spots in New York City charter schools performed better on state exams than students who entered the same lotteries but did not secure a charter school seat. By the third grade, according to the study, the average charter school student was 5.3 points ahead on state exams in English compared with students who were not admitted to the charter schools. In math, the students were 5.8 points ahead. It also found that students who attended a charter school from kindergarten to eighth grade nearly matched the performance of their peers in affluent suburban communities on state math exams by the time they entered high school—a phenomenon Caroline characterized as closing the "Harlem-Scarsdale" achievement gap. The results were somewhat less striking in English, where students closed 66 percent of the gap, according to the study.

The study gained attention in the media and filled us with a renewed sense of optimism and energy. And it proved to us what we'd understood all along: despite all the concerns that divided people over charter schools, the real discussion that needed to be taking place was not about politics, but about *children*.

––––

At the end of 2006, we came to the realization that if the Charter Center was going to be a strong and effective voice in terms of advocacy, we were going to have to make some internal changes. One of our best early moves had been hiring Matt Candler as COO. If Paula Gavin was hurt at times by her lack of background in the charter movement, Matt filled in those gaps and more. He studied charter schools at the Kellogg School of Management and then worked in the trenches, serving as co-principal of a newly established charter school in North Carolina. He later served as vice president of school development for the KIPP Foundation.

But in 2006, the year after Hurricane Katrina devastated New Orleans, Matt was hired away from us and went to work as the CEO of New Schools for New Orleans. We could hardly blame him. This was a great chance for him to put his belief in charter schools into practical application, replicating the work we had done at the Charter Center with more people and some fresh ideas. Paula Gavin had gotten the center off to a great start, but she needed to be replaced by someone with a deeper knowledge of public schools. She was energetic and committed, but she didn't have educational background, and without Matt there to help, we really did not have enough char-

ter school expertise in our leadership. Also, most of the people starting charter schools and CMOs were in their twenties and thirties
and had experience in education, often as Teach For America corps
members. Having a CEO without an education background created
a difficult situation for us.

The same dynamic applied as well to Joe, who was over seventy
by this time. He was ready to step down as chair and wanted the
board to replace him with Phoebe Boyer. He had a difficult time
with some of the board, who were wary of selecting not only a
woman but a young woman (shades of my own experience at the
Lexington School for the Deaf). A compromise was reached, and
Phoebe was designated to lead the search, in 2007, for Paula's replacement. She did an extraordinary job, attracting James Merriman, who had been the head of the SUNY Charter School Institute
and a real expert on the charter world, both in New York and nationwide. After Phoebe's handling of the search, the board was convinced that she was more than qualified to succeed Joe as chair. She
had the contacts outside of New York and the energy to lead the
organization, and indeed she has done a superb job ever since.

James went on to take the Center far beyond our original vision
of what it could do and what challenges it would face. He brought a
savvy and canny awareness to the role. When we started the Charter
Center in New York, we were the first—and only—such institution
anywhere in the country. Eventually, New Orleans, Nashville, Ten-
nessee, and Newark would follow suit, all borrowing heavily from
the model we had created.

With James and Phoebe in place, and us now in our seventies, we
were ready to finally retire *again* (although we did remain on the
board of the Beginning with Children Foundation for another three
years.)

Joe's public swan song was a speech to the New York charter summit in 2007. "As the oldest member of the New York charter

community, along with my young wife, Carol, I thought a moment of history of our effort in New York would be interesting to you," Joe said. "We started work on a charter-like school in 1989 and finally opened in 1992. We worked with the people at the Center for Educational Innovation, then part of the Manhattan Institute, whose leaders were early champions of school choice for parents who could not afford private schools. . . . We met with those leaders at the Manhattan Institute who told us, 'Our real goal is vouchers. Charters are all we could get. If you want the charter movement to be successful, get as far away from us as possible, and you will know you have been successful when a Democrat signs up and is willing to take on the entrenched opposition to change and reform.'

"We never dreamed that our Charter Center would not only receive the blessing of the new chancellor but his active participation and support. New York is now the national leader in charter reform, and our work is being copied in many cities nationwide—but nowhere with the support we have received from the mayor and the chancellor. I guess you can judge your success by the ferocity of your opposition, and we learned that the hard way last year when the assembly denied lifting the cap on the number of charters in New York. But they did not reckon with the new allies we had acquired. When the new Democratic Governor Eliot Spitzer endorsed the cap lift, and strong leaders like David Paterson and Malcolm Smith championed our cause, our opponents could no longer call this a white Republican fringe movement."

———

Joe and I were very much looking forward to finally heading into retirement, but it was shortly after this "retirement" began that we realized the idea had been premature. But it wasn't the Charter Center that drew us back to work—it was Beginning with Children Charter School. We knew that the development of a new school follows in its trajectory the uneven curve of human development. It has periods of acceleration, decline, adolescence and consolidation. The story of Beginning with Children Charter School follows this alternating pattern. Clearly the school was in a period of operational and academic decline, and this called for immediate action to reverse the trajectory. The school, then fifteen years old, was experiencing some serious growing pains that forced us to take action and get directly involved again. A number of choices had been made that did not work out well, and the net result was chaos. The school was doing well, but not stellar. The most recent scores showed that 69 percent of students in grades three to eight scored at or above grade level on the state English exam, compared with the 56 percent citywide average. And 77 percent of students scored at or above grade level on the math exam, compared with 65 percent citywide. These numbers were good, but for us they were not good enough for our children.

We knew that a lot of the problems the school faced stemmed from how it was being managed. Joe, Sonia, and I had stopped being as intimately involved as we had been from the beginning. Sonia announced her retirement for June 2003, and the board, after an exhaustive, nationwide search, found a principal to replace her. Before long, the board realized this replacement was not equipped to maintain the standards previously set for the school. Mimi Corcoran, executive director of the Beginning with Children Foundation, made the decision to promote one of the school's star teachers to the job of principal in 2004, a choice that fit with the school's commitment to making our teachers feel empowered. We had hoped that the other teachers at Beginning with Children would view the decision this way, but that did not happen. Instead, jealousies and infighting ensued.

The problem was exacerbated by a well-meaning but naive decision we had made when we converted the school into a charter school. Because we had designed our board to give voice to the various constituencies involved, including parents and teachers, the teachers on the board ended up essentially evaluating their boss—a potentially volatile situation. Rather than working to put aside their parochial concerns and looking to the larger picture of what was best for everyone, the board became shrill and factionalized. Meetings became an embarrassment. The board could not agree on even basic points, such as the nomination of a community board member. The incessant disagreement was so distracting that the board never succeeded in even working through all its agenda items at a given monthly meeting.

The verdict was clear: this dynamic had compromised the ability of the board to achieve satisfactory results for our students. But no good solutions presented themselves. It was as if the school had run into a dead end but could not back out. One of Mimi Corcoran's sons had developed a serious health issue and she would soon retire. She had tried bringing in conflict-resolution specialists to break the logjam with the board, but they made no progress. Meanwhile, the school's budget had taken a turn for the worse. As a unionized charter, we were responsible for pension benefits that had been growing astronomically.

We were asked by the Beginning with Children Foundation board to come in and try to resolve the impasse. Carol and I had immediate reservations about this idea. But John Day, the retired Pfizer executive who chaired the board, told us we needed to get involved because the conflict had sprawled beyond his capability to resolve it. John had worked well with Sonia in her days as principal, back when he was the Pfizer plant manager, so if he thought the situation was out of control, we knew it was. The more we thought about the mess that had developed with the board, the more it seemed clear to us both that we would have to get involved, and that strong action would need to be taken.

We decided that the school had to have a board whose members were all working in the interests of the children, and not preoccupied with pleasing the faction that had appointed them. Change was not going to come easy. We had few illusions about how turbulent the coming transition would be. Carol and I decided that if the board insisted on maintaining its flawed structure, knowing that this course would endanger the financial health of the school and jeopardize its future, then the time had come for the Beginning with Children Foundation and the two of us to walk away from the school for good.

We addressed the board on May 17, 2007, at one of its public meetings and outlined our position, but we made little headway. The opposition was led by a teacher named Gail Sims Bliss, who would lose her board seat if our proposal was carried out. Gail was allied with a parent, Karl Klingbeil. Klingbeil was well educated and a representative of the newly gentrified Williamsburg, which was no longer the dead zone of twenty years earlier. He wanted the school's educational program to be oriented more toward a gifted and talented curriculum. This sounded fine in theory, but in practice it would sacrifice the needs of the less advanced children we had set out to serve, and who still made up the majority of the student body. We followed up with a letter on May 22, 2007 to all members of the board.

"As the founders, we brought financial resources and relationships, and you—our families—brought wonderful children and a determination to work together to make a difference," we wrote. "When others told us we should have a high school, we were steadfast and insisted that we needed to start much earlier to make a difference. You trusted us. Over these many years we have kept our promises to each other. But today, we are worried that the school is not delivering on the promise we made together, so many years ago, to be the best and to make a real difference in our children's lives. You are a board that no longer works together and has been unable to make decisions on important issues. Various representative board members are fighting each other."

We went on to call for a board whose makeup would be skills-based, not constituency-based. This would be a major transformation, and to achieve it we called on every board member to resign.

"We ask that together we make a change," we wrote. "Together we must willingly move from the current board structure to one that reflects and supports the dynamic growth and development of the school. . . . We understand that the board may choose not to take this action. That being said, if the current board, at its meeting on May 24, does not vote to reconstitute to a skills-based structure, we will consider this the school's choice to sever the long-standing relationship between us personally and the school, and we will no longer provide financial support. In addition, we will recommend to the Beginning with Children Foundation Board of Trustees, at its next meeting on June 12, 2007, that it no longer participate as a partner organization with the school. Further, if this were to be the Beginning with Children Charter School Board's decision, the foundation would inform the appropriate regulatory authorities of the change. We would also ask the board to designate its representative to receive the books and records of the school."

We knew that if we were not firm in our position, the situation could quickly spin out of control. We did not attend the May 24 meeting because we were out of town at our grandson's bar mitzvah. We learned later that after a heated and unpleasant discussion, every board member but two (who represented the community) resigned. We also learned that a *New York Times* reporter had been invited to attend the meeting. We wondered why this seemingly insignificant squabble was of interest to anyone outside of the school community. Later, when the reporter, David M. Herszenhorn, called us and asked us some questions, we still were confused as to why he was even interested in this minor governance issue.

We were skeptical that anything would ever appear in the paper, but we kept scanning the Metro section to see if an article had appeared. Nothing did. Herszenhorn continued to call us with follow-up questions, but weeks passed and we assumed the story had been dropped. How wrong we were! Five weeks later, on June 28, we made our daily early morning scan of the Metro section and, again, happily found no story. The phone rang at 7:15 a.m., and it was Steve Kay, a good friend from Boston.

"Wow, that is quite a story about the two of you in the *Times* today!" he said.

We wondered why the *Times* would print the story in Boston and not in New York. After all, we had already checked the Metro section.

"Metro section?" Steve said. "You guys are on page one!"

That we were. We still cannot believe such an article was published. Entitled "Patrons' Sway Leads to Friction in Charter School," the article went into great detail about the problems at the school. It stated that we had forced most of the school's trustees to resign, threatening to cut our ties with the school and withdraw our financial support as part of a push for better student achievement. "At a board meeting last month," Herszenhorn wrote, "parents lashed out at the Reiches, angrily describing their relationship as that of master and servant or landlord and tenant." He also wrote that "the clash has exposed fault lines of wealth and class that are perhaps inevitable as philanthropists, in New York and nationwide, increasingly invest in public education, providing new schools to children in poor neighborhoods while making communities dependent on their generosity." Both Bliss and Klingbeil were quoted by Herszenhorn in the article, and someone, without consent of parents or the principal, let a *New York Times* photographer into the schools.

The article went on to declare:

> In educational philanthropy, the Reiches were pioneers. They fought for years to get the city's Board of Education to let them open the Beginning with Children school in 1992 in an impoverished section of Williamsburg, before charter schools became a national trend and at a time when private donors were generally reluctant to write checks to public school systems. The school converted to charter status in 2001. They fought through bureaucratic tangles to get the system to accept a virtually free building, a former Pfizer pharmaceutical factory, which the school now occupies for $1 a year. The school has done well, though far from stellar. . . . The state reauthorized the school's charter last year, giving it a full five-year renewal."

Overall, the tone was clearly of an editorial disguised as a news article. We were mortified. How could this be front-page news? How could a five-week-old minor squabble in a Brooklyn school push two wars and the heated upcoming presidential campaign to the inside pages of the paper? The story was slanted, inaccurate, and incomplete. We had worked hard in the Williamsburg community for twenty years to overcome the anti-Semitism prevalent there, and Herszenhorn used quotes that portrayed us as mere wealthy interlopers. The thousands of hours and millions of dollars we had invested in the children of that community were ignored. Our "crime" was an unwillingness to continue investing in an organization whose board was not structured to lead the school and serve the children properly. We had never sought publicity for the work we did, and we did not expect this. We heard from friends around the world and gained even more respect for Joel Klein: he told us that he ignored drivel like this and continued to do his job, and he advised us to do the same; it was a searing, painful experience. We kept saying to ourselves, "Keep your eyes and hearts on the children."

There was an amusing sidelight. Knowing how hard I had worked to gain my PhD, Joe wrote to Herszenhorn complaining of his failure to refer to me as Dr. Reich. Herszenhorn in his reply, lauded his article as "an extremely important window into issues related to private philanthropy in public schools." He then cited the N.Y. Times Manual of Style which said "Dr. should be used in all references for physicians and dentists whose practice is their primary current occupation . . . Anyone else with an earned doctorate, like a PhD degree may request the title but only if it is germane to the holder's current occupation." Noting that we had never objected to prior references of me as Mrs. Reich, he suggested that Joe's note had more to do with our general reaction to the article which he understood we viewed "as some sort of attack" than it did with his failure to use an honorific title. He concluded by sending thanks and regards to Joe "and to Dr. Reich as well."

Whatever our view of the article, David Herszenhorn's superiors at the newspaper apparently liked it. Soon after the article appeared, he was moved to the Washington desk, a big step up from the education desk.

# TWELVE

# BUILDING A MOVEMENT

## *JOE*

By 2006, the charter school movement had finally gained the momentum we'd hoped it could when we established the Charter Center two years earlier. In those two years, we had helped facilitate the opening of several charter schools, and it seemed like it was just the beginning. With the chancellor's success in attracting many CMOs to New York City, and the implementation of shared space, more and more people were coming to us with an interest in creating charter schools in their community. The problem, however, was that the original charter law had set a cap of one hundred charter schools—fifty in the state, and fifty in New York City—that could be authorized. Unless the cap was raised in the 2006 session of the legislature, dozens of applicants who had applied to start schools during the next two years would have to be turned away. It was time to make a major effort in Albany to raise the cap. Governor Pataki was in the final year of his third term. With nothing like a pay increase to trade with the Assembly, we had to convince them to act on the merits of our issue. A group of us organized a meeting with the Speaker of the New York State Assembly, Sheldon Silver, to push for the cap lift. We knew Silver could deliver the Democratic majority in the assembly and that he was not a fan of charter schools. He rarely, if ever, went against the wishes of the teachers' union, but nonetheless, we needed Silver's support if we were going to change the law, and we arrived at his New York office hoping for a miracle.

Instead, he nearly laughed us out of the room. "Very few of my members care about this issue," Silver said. We read between the lines: Democratic politicians relied on donations from the teachers' unions and they were deathly afraid of doing anything to cut off the flow of cash. Unfortunately, no lift of the cap occurred that year and, as a result, many of the charter management organizations who were hoping to bring educational choice to more New York City neighborhoods began to look elsewhere for their expansion.

This blow served as a wake-up call to the charter movement. A strong advocacy effort was imperative, and to succeed, it had to be accompanied by increased political spending. A much stronger advocacy effort was imperative. With the election of Eliot Spitzer as governor of New York in 2006, our chances improved greatly. He had a deep and sincere interest in improving education, had studied the issue for several years, and had become an ardent supporter of educational reform. His overwhelming win on Election Day, and unflagging support, made the lift on the charter schools cap a real possibility in 2007. We had developed a very good relationship with Eliot, who was way ahead of his party on the reform issue. We often speculated on how far he could have advanced school reform in New York State (and across the country) had his tragic downfall not occurred.

After 2006, Chancellor Klein became determined to match the union in advocacy and neutralize Speaker Silver, who was, in his view, our most powerful enemy. A big part of that effort was led by an organization called Democrats for Education Reform (DFER), whose intent was to give a voice to Democrats who wanted to end the unions' domination of the Democratic Party's approach to education. This goal had been a high priority of ours for years, but we had not had much time to work on it ourselves. But the political landscape needed to shift. It was time.

DFER's beginnings were modest enough. We had met John Petry, one of the founders of the group, in March 2005, and he'd told us about the formation of DFER and also asked for our help. We wanted to be supportive but had no illusions about the lack of support among Democrats when it came to the fight for educational choice.

"You can hold your national convention right here," I had told John at the time. "In our broom closet."

"Or in a phone booth," Carol said.

All the members of DFER would have fit in either place. They had no staff in those days and were a long way from becoming an effective advocacy organization that politicians would take seriously. That all changed, however, when Joe Williams joined the group in 2007, as executive director. Joe had labored in the trenches as an education reporter for the *New York Daily News*. That paper was head and shoulders above the *New York Times* in its reporting on charters, but Joe found his editors were often reluctant to give issues such as teacher training and the importance of pre-kindergarten education the coverage they clearly deserved—and would be increasingly getting in the years to come, as these issues rose to national prominence.

"I failed miserably trying to get these stories by my editors," Williams told the Pew Seminar on Early Childhood Education at Columbia University's Teachers College in May 2006.

Williams started to look for other ways to make a difference. He authored the book *Cheating Our Kids: How Politics and Greed Ruin Education*. He wrote in the preface to that book:

> As an education reporter on the nation's largest school system, I've observed firsthand some of the best and worst the public education has to offer. As a parent of two boys in New York City's public schools, I've felt the joys that fill a family's home when things are going well at school, along with the utter frustration that comes when conditions are less than perfect. By any reasonable standard, these are gloomy days for public education, but it doesn't have to be this way. My hope is that this book will contribute to the ongoing discussions about how the public can take back its schools in a way that puts children first in line for the system's attention.

Joe was well equipped to move DFER toward greater effectiveness. He knew firsthand how difficult it could be to get major newspapers to cover the revolution taking place in education through the charter school movement. He was press savvy and politically smart— what every good advocacy organization needs in a leader—and he banded together with people who knew what they were doing and had resources. The organization built a strong board of directors, including people like John Petry, Whitney Tilson, and Boykin Curry, all white "hedgies" very actively involved in DFER and other CMOs.

We had expected the United Federation of Teachers to feel a bit threatened by DFER's work, but we underestimated just how much this would be so. In December 2010, the UFT published an over-the-top attack on Joe Williams's group on its Web site, and it was almost comical in its excess.

The headline read: "Who Are Democrats for Education Reform? And Why Do They Keep Bashing Public Schools and Unions?"

Continuing in a question-and-answer style, the article went on to make such provocative queries as, "Why do Democrats for Education Reform hate teachers?"

Of course, the unions weren't going to like what was happening—it was forcing them to confront a stark new reality. They came into existence and gained their strength at a time, post-war, when there was an acute need for what they offered. At that time, they were righting a serious wrong in American society: the exploitation of female professionals who were effectively barred from every profession but teaching and thus were underpaid because they had no alternative and were not organized. The unions gave them representation and a series of benefits that were then common in the private sector and in universities—foremost among them incredibly generous pension benefits and near-certain lifetime tenure after three years.

At the same time that the unions gained these benefits, negotiating with incompetent bureaucracies and controlling state legislatures, other professions were opening their doors to women. Many women who in our generation would have become teachers were now becoming lawyers, physicians, architects, and business leaders. As a result, the teaching profession no longer had the direct line it once had on attracting the best and the brightest. Everyone who studies education's problems agrees the most important challenge is to enhance the stature and quality of the teaching profession. This way it can attract more of the individuals who are now going into other fields, where they are evaluated and compensated on performance, not on seniority or how many courses they took at schools of education. Sadly, that goal has become much harder to achieve. The acrimony among people in education only worsened when the 2008 recession added significant fiscal pressures to states and municipalities. This caused them to take a hard look, often for the first time, at the extraordinarily generous benefit structure that had been gained for public employees by their unions, who had out-negotiated their employers for decades. Why should employers negotiate aggressively when they knew that governors and mayors wouldn't back them, since any political pain would be immediate and carry long-term consequences?

Part of the new reality for the unions arose when President Barack Obama was elected on a platform that included supporting charter schools. Obama had also been an early supporter of Democrats for Education Reform. As far back as 2004, when he was a little-known state legislator in Illinois running for the United States Senate, Obama declared that he supported "new opportunities for charter schools." Running for president in 2008, he vowed during a September speech in Ohio that as president, he would "double the funding for responsible charter schools." Once he took office, Obama did not forget these promises. He appointed Arne Duncan, a long-time educational reformer, as the Secretary of Education. Duncan was raised in the Hyde Park neighborhood of Chicago; both of his parents were educators, and he attended the same University of Chicago Laboratory School that Carol had. Duncan was a strong advocate for charter schools during his time as CEO of Chicago Public Schools, which started in 2001. Equally as significant, Duncan, once a co-captain of the Harvard basketball team, was a personal friend of Obama's, making continuing access likely.

The most significant piece of education legislation during Obama's first term was called Race to the Top, and it was very supportive of charters. It elaborated on a variety of criteria that schools would have to meet to be eligible for funding through the program, and aimed to support high-performing charter schools and other innovative schools. In a September 27, 2010, interview with *The Today Show*'s Matt Lauer highlighting Race to the Top, Obama emphasized that the administration also intended to close the poorest-performing 5 percent of schools in the nation and turn some of them into charter schools.

"Charter schools are not a panacea," the president said. "Reform is hard, it's systematic, it takes time, but we know that there are some charters who have figured out how to do a very good job in the lowest-income schools with the kids who are two, three grade levels behind, and yet they can achieve 90, 95 percent graduation rates, boost reading scores and math scores very high. What we've got to do is to look at the success of these schools, find out how do we duplicate them, and make sure that we are still holding charter schools accountable, the same way we are with all the schools. We shouldn't say just because a school is a charter that it's an excellent school, because there's some actually very poor-performing charters. But what I'm interested in, what my secretary of education (sic) are interested in, is fostering these laboratories of excellence where we start learning."

There it was! The word *laboratory*. It had been spoken out loud in the context of charter schools from a visible and prominent platform. Finally!

All of us in the charter movement were thrilled by this interview. It seemed that the time had finally come where fresh thinking and hard work had shifted the political ground to where the teachers' unions' stranglehold on the Democratic Party was finally slipping. Democrats were beginning to regain their bearings after having lost their way on the issue. Long known for being dependable champions of the rights of minorities, the Democrats had been led astray. They followed union leadership into the questionable choice of opposing school reform.

In the ensuing years, we have watched with a lot of interest how the unions' aggressive response to these issues has altered the public's view of teachers and teachers' unions. Where previously teachers and unions were held with equal regard, unions are now seen less favorably than teachers. There also seems to be a movement among teachers to distance themselves from policies that are designed to protect adults and ignore the needs of children.

––––––

In recent years, several other issues have escalated from an occasional skirmish into continuous battles, where compromise and moderation have become less possible. Mayoral control of education, which had been granted to New York by the legislature in 2002, came with a sunset clause calling for it to expire in June 2009. Mayor Bloomberg then decided to run for a third term, overturning the term limits by a vote of the city council. Term limits had been originally imposed by popular vote, and many people felt the mayor should have held a popular vote to overturn them. This action, coupled with the mayor's disregard for many of the checks and balances built into the law, produced a backlash that threatened to revoke mayoral control of education. Whatever the flaws in the new system, we realized a return to the old Board of Education would be a major step backward. The mayor won this battle with only minor cosmetic changes to his authority, but in the process he lost some of his support.

On April 1, 2009, Regent Merryl H. Tisch was named Chancellor of the Board of Regents. The assembly's control of the regents had been very important to Speaker Silver's domination of educational policy in the state. Merryl's ascension to Chancellor effectively served notice that the Speaker was no longer going to consistently stand in the way of change. Richard P. Mills, who had been the State's Commissioner of Education for thirteen years and had been largely invisible, announced in October, 2008 that he would retire on

June 30, 2009. The State Education Department did nothing under Mill's leadership except burnish its reputation as the most inept and ineffectual of the state's many sorry agencies. Merryl had gained the support of both Speaker Silver and her fellow regents over the years with her hard work and focus on important issues. On July 27, 2009 the Regents named Dr. David M. Steiner, the talented and respected dean of the Hunter College School of Education as Mills's successor. Steiner's senior deputy was Dr. John B. King Jr., a veteran charter leader. These moves changed the landscape for charters in a positive way. If there was union opposition to these appointments, it was not visible.

The importance of these changes quickly became apparent. Arne Duncan had announced that Race to the Top was offering a very large pot of money to financially suffering states, but New York had taken a very casual approach to applying for this program. One requirement for application was to have a charter law that was not unduly restrictive; for New York, that would have meant enacting legislation to increase the cap on the number of charter schools allowable.

In June 2009, we went to North Carolina to attend a meeting of the James B. Hunt, Jr. Institute for Educational Leadership and Policy, an organization started by former Governor James B. Hunt, whose original board we had served on. Its purpose is to train governors and their staffs in education. This meeting would feature Secretary Duncan, who was going to announce the procedures for getting Race to the Top funds. There were more than twenty governors there, and every state that didn't send a governor sent its state education superintendent instead—every state, that is, except New York. Commissioner Mills was weeks away from retirement and his successor had not yet been named and Governor Paterson was not present. From what we heard, New York was relying on its two Democratic senators to gain funds for the state the old-fashioned way: through political influence. At this meeting it became clear that Secretary Duncan was going to follow a clear and transparent process, and that politics alone would not determine the winners. New York was not named in the first round.

The realization that inaction had cost New York $700 million in a time of budget shortfall moved the regents to action. Steiner and King put together a first-rate application. Although the union opposed some of the provisions and won some points, the 2010 cap lift passed. When Steiner stepped down in 2011 to return to Hunter College, King was named as his replacement. All of this was a great victory for reform.

Race to the Top brought education reform to the forefront of the debate over the United States's role in the global economy. Education had always been a state issue. States devised their own tests, and political pressure had caused the tests to be dumbed down to make the scores look better. There is a set of tests given nationally, called the National Assessment of Educational Progress (NAEP), that conforms to international standards. US students score much lower on NAEP than on state tests. When we compare our results with those of other countries, it's clear the United States is falling behind. The 2009 Programme for International Student Assessment (PISA) tests, which were given to fifteen-year-olds, rank the United States thirtieth in math, twenty-third in science, and seventh in reading. When the results are adjusted for income level, the United States fares quite differently: the wealthiest 10 percent of US students score first in the world.

The implications of this are horribly clear to us. Poverty is being used as an excuse for poor educational results. The success of many of the best charter schools proves that poverty can be overcome, and that poor test results reflect poor education and may be the cause of ongoing poverty rather than its result. Certainly the achievements of our Dreamers and the graduates of most of our charter schools show that greater educational opportunity produces more productive, accomplished citizens.

Data about New York State lobbying expenditures released in 2010 showed that the nonprofit Education Reform Now had outspent the teachers unions for the first time. Until the arrival of DFER, most reformers felt the righteousness of their cause would triumph and that there was no need to pay politicians to do what was right for their constituents. When we failed to get the cap on charters raised in 2006, we learned the harsh realities of state politics. Charter applications in New York City grew from twenty-five thousand in 2008 to one hundred fifteen thousand in 2011. Sadly, charter waiting lists by 2011 exceeded fifty thousand, more than the forty-five thousand students who were due to attend charter schools that school year.

The hard-line reformers argue that the union is serving the interests of its members and taking positions that do not serve children. The unions favor near-automatic lifetime tenure, oppose any accountability in determining teacher compensation, demand that "last in first out" be the sole basis for layoffs, and insist on maintaining a lucrative, defined-benefit pension system that is not available to others in our society. In the past few years, the reform movement has developed the skills and resources necessary to wage political war with the unions, and has raised public awareness of these issues.

The critics of reform still insist that demography defines destiny, and that children of poverty cannot close the achievement gap without the aid of massive social programs. So what is the truth? There are now more than two million students in charter schools. The movement has brought choice to millions of families to whom it had previously been denied, and they will not surrender that right no matter who is in power. The defenders of the status quo no longer hold a monopoly on education. In New York, Merryl Tisch's favored candidates for commissioners of education, both reformers, were approved without overt opposition. Even in Washington, DC, where Chancellor Michelle Rhee's aggressive and controversial reforms were the key issue in 2010's mayoral election, the new mayor nominated Rhee's deputy, Kaya Henderson, as the new chancellor.

So where do things stand today? It is hard to write about history while it is still being made, but there are some conclusions that we think are likely to survive. On the positive side, issues are now on the table that were unthinkable as recently as five years ago. These issues were brought to the forefront largely thanks to the charter movement's success. Choice and its accompanying accountability are now a reality for many thousands of children and families who previously lived without hope. Automatic tenure, teacher evaluation, training, and compensation are now being discussed. The recession has brought the excesses of public employees' pensions to light, and this issue has finally become a legitimate subject for debate.

Arguments about charter schools have become heated. The 2010 film *Waiting for Superman* was hailed as a way to get the public talking about education reform. But while it did show the trauma of the lottery required for charter schools, it also demonized the teachers' unions. We are long-standing admirers of Randi Weingarten, who was president of a New York chapter of the United Federation of Teachers for twelve years and is now leader of the American Federation of Teachers, the most progressive of the two national teachers' unions. Our admiration exists even though we disagree with her on most issues. It is our belief that she was way ahead of her union members on most issues and could not have continued to hold her job had she moved any faster. She tried to embrace change by having the UFT start a charter school in Brooklyn, building on the idea of charters as incubators started by her predecessor, Albert Shanker. While working on this book, we met with her to talk over our shared experiences. In our early struggle to open the school, it was Randi to whom we often turned for assistance in our struggle with the bureaucrats at the Board of Education. Carol said, "You have, from the beginning, been kind, reasonable, and often protective toward us—why did you do that?"

"Because you two were the real deal," she told us. "A lot of people in the charter movement talk about kids and may be really interested in helping kids. But they're equally interested in tearing things down. I never saw you interested in tearing things down or as an adversary. We just had a difference of opinion on many issues. You have to worry when you have this level of teacher bashing and demagoguery about teachers. You have a worse situation because of this intense polarization. I saw the two of you as people who really wanted change for the benefit of kids, combining Joe's business experience and Carol's school cred and the emotional, psychological, pedagogical stuff."

"But we didn't know anything," Carol protested.

"I don't think that," Randi said, laughing, perhaps recalling how, ten years earlier, we had compared her union to the United Auto Workers and the charter movement to Toyota, or a noisy argument she'd had with us and Mimi Corcoran about the lunacy of the union contract.

Even Randi's sternest critics must feel a touch of remorse now that they're dealing with her UFT successor, Michael Mulgrew, who has escalated the battle between unions and the reform movement. A sad example of this vitriol can be found in Mulgrew's 2011 suit, on behalf of the teachers' unions, against the New York Department of Education, which attempted to block the city from closing twenty-two poorly performing schools and placing charter schools in fifteen of these buildings that would be partially vacated by the closures. This, to us, was a classic case of turning everything into a turf war instead of thinking about what is best for the kids. But what we could not begin to fathom was why the National Association for the Advancement of Colored People (NAACP) would join the opposition and get involved in this and other similar lawsuits.

As summarized in a July 21, 2011, article in the *New York Times*, a paper with a history of hostility toward the charter movement, "The lawsuit rose to national attention over the last two months, largely because of the NAACP's involvement. Critics charged that the civil rights organization was on the wrong side of the charter school issue because in New York City, many high-performing charter schools serve mostly black students."

It was not just critics making this charge. It was also the parents of the students. They wanted charter schools to give their kids a shot at a better future, and here the NAACP was stepping in to try to deny them that hope? It was incredible.

Then it got worse. A charter school parent named Janette Ramos sent an e-mail to Dr. Hazel N. Dukes, the president of the NAACP New York State Conference, asking the NAACP to withdraw from this lawsuit, and Dukes responded with an e-mail that could hardly have been more inflammatory.

"You are not a member of the NAACP and don't understand that you are doing the business of slave masters," she wrote.

The people who have gained most from charter schools in New York have been African-Americans and Latinos. We found it outrageous that a political leader would use such language, and we were not alone. As the *New York Daily News* reported, on June 7, 2011:

Ramos, a hospital administrator whose son is a kindergartner at Bronx Success Academy Charter School, said she was infuriated by Dukes's response to her email.

"She's trying to intimidate me,' said Ramos, who is Puerto Rican. "I am a minority —I'm in the same boat as everyone else. I'm just trying to (sic) the best job for my kids."

Dukes and the NAACP were not going to shift their biased, poorly conceived opposition to charters, no matter how many minority parents told the organization just how wrong they were. We thought Dukes did tremendous damage to her cause with her clumsy advocacy, and Joel Klein agreed with that assessment.

"I was shocked by that," Joel told us. "The NAACP made a huge mistake. I mean, they get killed over this thing, because they're blocking seven thousand families of color. These are real people. This is not about school closure or anything. So I think this is World War III, and I think they're going to lose. Now even they know they're going to lose. They want out of it. They don't know how to get out of it gracefully."

Today there are seven thousand families waiting for their children to attend these schools, and the NAACP and the UFT want to fight against shared space in underutilized New York City public school buildings. These families just want to exercise their right as citizens to choose what they see as a preferable placement for their children. The lawsuit works against the futures of historically underserved children, in the name of what? Unless everyone remembers that, as educators, we serve children and their families, we will be robbing ourselves of an independent future. There is nothing so frightening to those in power as an educated, thinking population that's determined to act. These critical voters will emerge slowly and in small numbers unless they are spurred to action. The bureaucrats' fear, however conscious, of an organized emergence of such a population may well have been what doomed our community center a decade ago, and still stands in the way of properly educating our neediest children. It is startling to consider that John Dewey, a founder of progressive education, was also a founding member of both the NAACP and the American Civil Liberties Union—both now on the attack and playing the race card.

The reform movement is changing, too. Joel Klein and Michelle Rhee, no longer constrained by their official positions in the school system, are taking a much more aggressive stance toward unions and legislators supporting the unions' position. They have been joined by a legion of new reform advocates, most of them from the financial community, who view this struggle as all-out war and are providing the financial resources to match the union effort. Eva Moskowitz, founder of the rapidly growing Success Academy Charter Schools and former chair of the New York City Council Education Committee, is aggressively organizing the parents in her schools and pushing the envelope on the role of charters. Whereas charters have heretofore primarily served children of poverty who had no choice, Eva has begun to open charters in middle-class neighborhoods that are also badly underserved by the current system. The unions, meanwhile, have vigorously opposed her efforts to gain shared space. With the 2013 mayoral election likely to produce a Democratic mayor supported by the teachers' union, education reform seems likely to join other major political disagreements in current US politics, where the extremists dominate the debate and moderates have no forum.

One voice of moderation is that of James Merriman, the CEO of the Charter Center we helped establish. James is someone with experience, knowledge, and vision. He recently outlined his perspective to us on the challenges facing the Center and the charter movement in the coming years:

"We do have to answer some criticisms of the charter movement that are substantive and reasonable, even if we don't like where they come from," he said. "When we were a bit player, it was fine to start schools when we want, where we want, how we want. Just the fact of their existence was enough. But that changes as charters are sitting in public school space, are replacing other public schools, and seen as an alternative to other public schools. As we get larger in numbers and in the amount of money transferring over from the district to charters, we become something significant, now amounting to hundreds of millions of dollars a year. In Harlem, in Central Brooklyn, in the South Bronx, there is a concentration of schools where it's certainly possible that one in three kids in kindergarten will be in a charter school. Issues around who we are serving and how we're serving them become legitimate issues.

"The teachers' union has absolutely been able to make inroads around that and put questions in a lot of people's minds about whether charter school success was simply a question of demographics. I don't think it is. I think the Hoxby study shows that it's more than demographics that account for differences in test scores. But I am convinced that if we are going to exist in public school space we need to serve more English Language Learner kids [whose first language is not English], as well as more kids with special education needs, and a wider range of them.

"These are the issues. The politics have profoundly changed. No one thinks that they are going to strangle the charter movement in the cradle. We are no longer in the cradle. That's my point about growing up: if you want to sit at the adult table, then you have to act like adults. But a lot of Democrats in office are deeply concerned about English Language Learners and the special needs issue, both from their honest sense of what good policy is as well as their sense of the politics of the issue. That becomes: 'Look guys, unless you solve this, you really are vulnerable to these charges, and it's hard to defend a set of public schools run essentially with a set of different rules around accessibility.'

"The inability to get beyond that doesn't allow us to have conversations about what is good about charters and so forth. So I think it's important we address those issues. I also think it's critically important that we start talking about the transference of what's working in charters or what's working in districts between the sectors. The politicians desperately want to see that because their basic calculation was this: 'Look, I have a lot of kids in charters and they're happy and the parents love them and they're happy. But a lot of parents have kids who aren't in them and they're unhappy because they see someone getting a goodie that they don't have and they don't like it.' They are asking for some political cover. It's precisely because the Charter Center is not a membership organization that we are able to lead this discussion. I have to get charters behind me, but I don't have to count votes or worry that one group might get other charters upset, which would lead to a management issue. The Center has a unique position as both a spur to policy initiatives and as a grantor of funds if we turn the conversation from one of charter versus district into one of good schools, whether they are charter or district. We need to say that we're agnostic about the form the school takes as long as it's good. If we can take those steps, then we become much more politically palatable."

The issues in reform now go beyond charter schools, which were primarily responsible for bringing them into the spotlight. One of our mentors, Deborah Meier, warned us when we were starting out that our work ran the risk of being a footnote in the history of education reform. In this case, we believe she was wrong. The charter movement we helped birth will endure." Now that millions of children and families have experienced choice where there once was none, the clock will not be turned back to the days of the dead zone, when an excellent education was available only to the privileged few. If the two sides now warring find common ground, American public education will be permanently changed for the better and be more about serving children and learning. If the current militancy continues, and the education system continues to favor the adults who work in it, an educated populace will not emerge, and our country will continue to slip internationally.

# EPILOGUE

## JOE AND CAROL

Carol's brother died in June 1995. Carol had been asked to speak on behalf of the family at the service, and that morning, they gathered in the back of the National War College auditorium, in Washington, DC, waiting for people to arrive and take their seats. The journalist Cokie Roberts was there—she and her family were good friends of Carol's brother's family—and after spotting Carol in the back, she came over and took Carol's hands in hers.

"This is what you must understand now, and when you go out there to speak," Cokie said. "You are the resident memory of your family now." These words have stuck with Carol all of these years, and we are especially reminded of them today. In many ways, we are the resident memory of New York City's charter school movement, having been involved with it since the beginning. And in thinking about what memory best encapsulates the work of the last twenty-five years, one specific story comes to both of our minds, quite vividly.

It was the evening of June 17, 2010, and we were standing on the dais in a banquet room at New York City's Plaza Hotel. We had mixed feelings about being honored by the Beginning with Children Foundation, which we ourselves had founded. Through the years, we've chosen to do what we can to avoid the spotlight. But sometimes ceremonies help us look back on our lives with clarity. That's what happened that night at the Plaza, as we began to get a sense of what had been accomplished in opening our first school in Brooklyn, and in taking the fight for charter schools from there.

"The Beginning with Children School was the first charter-like school in our city," Mayor Bloomberg told the gathering that evening. "Its results were so heartening that Joe, Carol, and the Foundation then fought to make charter schools legal in New York State, so even more students and parents could benefit from choice and accountability in public education. They've been champions for our schools ever since. Their work helped pass the charter law in 1998. They played a big role in creating the New York City Charter School Center in 2004. And their support was instrumental in raising the state cap on charter schools in 2007, in extending mayoral control over the schools in 2009, and in spurring New York State's Race to the Top efforts this year. . . . So much of our reform agenda has begun with the work that Carol and Joe pioneered."

As we listened to Mayor Bloomberg and Chancellor Klein speak that night, each of us found ourselves reflecting on the amazing change that had taken place in education in our city during the past two decades. But it wasn't the speeches that night that brought it all home. It was the sight of the master of ceremonies: a handsome, clear-eyed young man named Omar Lopez.

Omar had been a member of our first kindergarten class at Beginning with Children, in 1992. He went on to attend Catholic High School, and then the College of Saint Rose in Albany, New York, where he became the first person of color to be elected student body president. Afterward, he attended the Harvard Graduate School of Education, on scholarship. After Harvard, Omar returned to the

Brooklyn community where he had gone to kindergarten. That evening, he announced he would start teaching in our Community Partnership Charter School in that fall. Later, he would go to work for DFER.

Being a part of Omar's life throughout the years, paying witness to the great success he's had in life and looking forward to the successes we know await him—all this is greater testament to the merits of the type of education we believe in than any story we could recall, or any message we might deliver. The movement is young. Omar started at Beginning with Children in 1992, six years before New York had a charter law. There are thousands of young people like Omar who have been beneficiaries of this movement that gave them hope where none had existed before moving through the system now. They will support this movement that gave them a choice and demand it for their children.

---

We think back to those early mornings when the Beginning with Children School began, and remember our custom of standing before a room full of children just like Omar and saying: "You can be anything you want to be, just finish school."

Over the years, we've come to learn this lesson for ourselves. At no point along the way did we ever truly know what was coming next. We were not experienced enough to predict our future accurately. We just knew that we were committed to expanding the opportunities for children in New York, especially those who lived in poverty, and we found our way from there. For us, the answer to poverty has always been education. We were led to this conclusion through different experiences. For me, Carol, it was because I was trained by my father, at the tender age of seven, to believe that I had a responsibility to make the world a better place—and, because of the great schooling I received, I believed education was the way to do it. As I grew older and began to pay more attention, I realized that in the decades that had passed since Brown v. Board of Education, nothing had really happened. Education reform efforts were focused on issues of race rather than education. Early on in our work, Joe met Annette Polly Williams, an African-American legislator from Milwaukee. I will never forget what she stood up and announced to a room one day: "I don't care about integration, I care about education. Let's distribute the education, not the kids." Her words have had a big impact on our efforts.

For me, Joe, my journey to this cause was a bit different. I've often been inspired by Carol, her determination and foresight. I will always remember that letter she wrote me when she was just twenty-one years old, reminding me that a life lived in pursuit of money might end up feeling empty. By remembering that advice, I was able to walk away from one very lucrative experience into a far more fulfilling one. Carol was blessed with a wonderful early education. I succeeded despite an inferior education in poor public schools. Yet I grew up in an environment where learning was valued, and that gave me a chance. I knew the children of Williamsburg faced a far greater challenge. For me, the goal was to be an agent of change and help the children we served achieve what Carol told them, each morning, was possible.

And we both shared a common and basic belief: families of means can afford to send their children to private schools or relocate to an affluent neighborhood where the public schools have greater resources. The poor cannot. We recoiled against this injustice. We made it our own struggle.

This tale began with the story of Ingrid and ends, in a way, with the story of Omar. But there are so many others with similar stories of achievement—achievement that the existing conditions in the dead zone would never have permitted. We had the idea that we could start a public school, something that had never been done by two private citizens. In our quest, we made many good decisions and lots of mistakes. And as we prepared to complete this book, and end this part of the story, we were blessed with a reminder of a decision made eighteen years ago.

In 1994, we were asked by Frank and Lourdes Putz, the parents of our student Amanda, to admit their son Jon to Beginning with Children. We had a policy of admitting siblings of existing students—a policy that later became part of the New York State Charter Law. Jon was a "special" child, born with Down Syndrome. Carol and Sonia spoke with his devoted and concerned parents and agreed to admit Jon, making it clear that if Jon failed to receive a good education, it would be the school's fault, not his. Jon did not fail. He completed his education and now works in a bookstore. Yesterday, we received a brochure announcing an art show that will be held in the bookstore. It will feature the art of Jon Putz, art inspired by the Muppets. The smiling face of Kermit is featured on the brochure— the same Kermit who was Carol's talisman while walking the streets of Williamsburg when starting the school!

Looking back now, we know that just because our idea—to start a public school, as private individuals—had never been done before, that was no reason not to do it. We proved we could make the seemingly impossible happen, just as Ingrid, Omar, and Jon have proved as well. After more than fifty years together, we now know that, with a little patience and a lot faith, you'll very likely find a little miracle waiting, in a form or shape you might never imagine, around every corner.

# CHARTER SCHOOLS BY THE NUMBERS

## CHARTER SCHOOLS IN NEW YORK CITY

According to the New York City Charter School Center, 23 charter schools were open at the time of Charter Center's founding in 2004. (Of these, 1 has subsequently closed.) Since the Charter Center was founded, an additional 117 have opened. (Of these, 3 have subsequently closed.)

As of January 2012, 136 charter schools operated in New York City. For the next two years, the New York City Charter School Center estimates 25 schools will open in the fall of 2012, and 19 will open in the fall of 2013.

There are 47,000 New York City students enrolled in charter schools.

Per-pupil funding from the New York City Department of Education: $13,527 (excludes federal, grant, in-kind, categorical, and privately donated resources).

In 2011, there were an estimated 64,000 applicants to city charter schools for an available 12,900 number of slots, leaving 51,100 students on wait lists.

Fourteen city charter schools, or 10 percent, have contracts or are negotiating contracts with the United Federation of Teachers union.

Programmatically, 6 schools have dual language programs, and 4 are single sex.

## Charter Enrollment by Demographics

62 percent African-American

31 percent Latino

76 percent free or reduced-price lunch

6 percent English Language Learners

13 percent special education

## Charter Schools by Network

60 are affiliated with nonprofit charter management organizations (CMOs)

12 are affiliated with for-profit educational management organizations (EMOs)

64 are independent charter schools

## Facilities

81 charter schools are in buildings owned by the New York City Department of Education

50 are in private space

5 have some students in shared space

## 2010–11 Achievement Data

|  | Charter Schools | District Schools |
|---|---|---|
| Math | 68% | 57% |
| ELA | 45% | 44% |

[NYC school percent of students at or above standards (NYS exams, Grades 3–8)]

## CHARTER SCHOOLS IN THE UNITED STATES

National numbers on charter schools, according to the National Center for Education Statistics:

- As of November 2010, charter schools operated in 40 states and the District of Columbia. In the following states, a charter school law has not been passed: Alabama, Kentucky, Maine, Montana, Nebraska, North Dakota, South Dakota, Vermont, Washington, and West Virginia.
- From 1999 to 2009, charter school enrollment nationwide went from 340,000 to 1.4 million.
- From 1999 to 2009, the percentage of public schools that were charter schools increased from 2 percent to 5 percent.
- During the 2008–09 school year, there were 4,700 charter schools in the United States.
- During the 2008–09 school year, 30 percent of charter schools were in high-poverty areas, compared to 19 percent of traditional public schools.
- Roughly 2 percent of students grades one through twelve were enrolled in a charter school in 2007, according to a statistical analysis report published in April 2010, analyzing data from 1993 to 2007.

- In 2007, roughly one-third of students had parents who considered enrolling them in a school other than the one they were currently attending.
- African-American and Asian students were most likely to have parents who had considered enrolling them in a school other than the one they were currently attending, with 45 percent of African-American students and 34 percent of Asian students having parents considering alternate schools.
- The higher the parents' level of education, the more likely the parent was to consider enrolling the student in a different school.
- A higher percentage of African-American students were enrolled in chosen public schools (charter and magnet schools) then were students of other races.
- More students from one-parent families attended chosen public schools (charter and magnet schools) than students from two-parent families.
- Students from the western United States were most likely to attend chosen public schools (charter and magnet schools), while students from the Northeast were least likely.
- Roughly half of charter school students were considered poor or near poor (coming from households with incomes less than 200 percent of the poverty threshold).
- The percentage of charter schools that were high-poverty schools—where 75 percent or more of students were eligible for free or reduced-price lunch (FRPL)—increased from 13 percent in 1999–2000 to 30 percent in 2008–09. In comparison, 19 percent of traditional public schools were considered high poverty in 2008–09. During this time period, the percentage of charter schools that were low poverty (25 percent of students or less were eligible for FRPL) decreased from 37 to 24 percent.

- In 2008–09, over half (54 percent) of charter schools were elementary schools, while secondary and combined schools accounted for 27 and 19 percent of charter schools, respectively. The distribution was different at traditional public schools: 71 percent were elementary schools, 24 percent were secondary schools, and 5 percent were combined schools. In 2008–09, about 55 percent of charter schools were located in cities, 21 percent were in suburban areas, 8 percent were in towns, and 16 percent were in rural areas. In contrast, 25 percent of traditional public schools were in cities, 28 percent were in suburban areas, 14 percent were in towns, and 33 percent were in rural areas.

- A higher percentage of parents reported being satisfied with the performance of their student's chosen public school (62 percent reported "very satisfied") than parents of students who attended an assigned public school (52 percent reported "very satisfied").

# ACKNOWLEDGMENTS

This story could never have happened without a great deal of support and trust. From the parents, especially the first ones who took a chance on two unknown strangers with their children. From the teachers and administrators in our schools and the staff at Beginning with Children Foundation who wanted something better for children, who shared our vision, and joined the struggle to make that vision real. From the Dreamers and the students in our schools whose accomplishments validated our belief in them and who became shining examples of what all children can achieve given the opportunity. From the leadership and staff at El Puente which welcomed us to the South Side, gave our program a home and found for us Gino Maldonado who became our Project Coordinator. From the generous individuals and foundations who provided the resources to make our ideas become real. Special thanks to the many supporters at Pfizer who bet on us, backed us in our travails, and never sought any credit for their efforts. Special thanks to our largest financial backer whose unquestioning support we have enjoyed for nearly 50 years in efforts both commercial and philanthropic who prefers to remain anonymous.

We also want to thank those visionaries who inspired us. Gene Lang, founder of I Have A Dream, who at 92, is still vigorously laboring to make the world a better place. He not only created a great program to serve children. He motivated many others to follow him who have multiplied Gene's impact many times over. And Joel Klein whose energy, passion for children, and guts made education reform a reality in New York City and showed the way for much of the United States. He took Mike Bloomberg's commitment to education and made it a reality inspiring talented newcomers to join the cause while bearing the abuse and resistance of the forces of the status quo. Also Jim Hunt, the former four time governor of North Carolina who not only made giant strides in education in his own state, but is now, through an Institute he created, helping governors nationally to deal with education reform. And those many entrepreneurs who are changing the face of NYC public education with their energy and creativity and who worked with the two of us.

A special thank you to two people who stood by our side from the beginning and are continuing the work. The first is Tracy Nagler who joined us in 1992 and has provided us with financial knowledge, general wisdom and guidance. She helped us to find new ways of doing things that aided our cause and stopped us from doing others which would have hurt it. And Sonia Gulardo, our founding principal who ran the Beginning with Children School for 12 years and has since gone on to create a truly amazing alumni program for her babies which has helped them through high school and college. Sonia was the face of our work to the community and beloved by the children and families she nurtured.

The story in this book is ours, and we bear full responsibility for its contents. Nevertheless, two novice authors could not have produced this without a lot of help. From Steve Kettmann who helped us create the first rendition of the book and introduced us to February Partners where we learned how to make what we had into a readable book. From Aimee Molloy who stepped in and turned our initial manuscript into this book. From the dozens of people who sat for interviews and brought old tales back to life. From Sandra Lerner who when we were stumped for a title, gave us the one we used. From the many friends who helped polish our several drafts with constructive commentary. From our three daughters Debby, Marcia and Janet whose existence along with the six grandchildren they gave us—Max, Amos, Corie, Hazel, Pearl & Asher—made us want to create a better world for all children. And from our assistant, Torri Oats who was there to lend loyalty, sanity and continuity to two senior citizens.